E.

The Bible is full of "military" metaphors. I have always been intrigued when I hear "soldiers" speak of their experiences to help me visualize the Scriptures. Brother Rangel does just that. From "boot camp" to "coming home" (whether by death, or retirement, or the end of a deployment) Brother Rangel describes the life of the soldier with definition of "military terms", and examples of soldiers in "action" to give a real life awareness of what it means to be in the Lord's Army. The illustrations of particular soldiers and their exploits give the book life. Brother Rangel gives great insight with the Scriptures of how to survive as a "Soldier" in the Lord's Army.

– David McCracken
International Evangelist

It has been my privilege to be Si Rangel's pastor for about twenty five years. His service to our country as a Green Beret, Paratrooper, Jump Master, and Sergeant Major has spanned decades. He completed a tour of duty in Afghanistan just prior to his sixtieth birthday. He has counted his service to the Lord as even more important than his service to his country. Si has been involved in the ministry of our church from very early on. He currently directs our Discipleship ministry and we recently had about twenty people recognized for the completion of discipleship training. He also is Director of our Local Church Bible Institute.

As he grew in his walk with the Lord he noticed more and more the parallels that existed in the principles that govern armies, military leaders and fighting men and the principles that govern Christians in the warfare the Bible reveals that we are in. Often we find we learn things on one level by observing them in another level. Our Saviour sometimes taught his own disciples truths that were spiritual and eternal by using ordinary things which the disciples better understood. Things like boats and fishing, seeds and farming, architects and building, money and banking, medicine and nursing, garments and clothing.

The soldier was a common presence in Israel in the time of our Lord's ministry on earth. He even had one among the twelve who had the mindset of a soldier, that in Simon the Zealot. When he taught the principle of authority, he used a soldier, a Centurion, to do it.

Si Rangel, in this book takes us through the life and times of the soldier and helps us recognize that all who are Christians are enlisted in God's army. Our challenge is to be a good soldier. Our comrades in arms are helped or hindered by our actions on the field of battle. Principles you learn in these pages will assist you to achieving your potential as one God can use, and one who can stand someday before the Captain of our salvation and receive the commendations given the good soldier.

– William Rench
Pastor, Calvary Baptist Church, Temecula, CA

My hope is that every Christian will read this powerful and life changing book. Si Rangel passionately opens our eyes to the reality of spiritual warfare and then brilliantly explains what we need to know and do in order to survive on the spiritual battlefield. Because it contains such valuable and necessary counsel to Christians, I will be recommending this book to everyone I know.

– Karen Center
Women's Counseling Ministry, Calvary Baptist Church, Temecula, CA

As a retired Fire Captain, I thoroughly enjoyed how Si Rangel was able to highlight the similarities between the Christian and military lifestyles. This book is an excellent tool to help equip the Christian soldier to fight those spiritual and physical battles that we all encounter. I highly recommend this book to everyone. However, I believe it's definitely a "must read" for anyone in the military or paramilitary, like Police and Fire.

– Vince Tosches
Fire Captain (Ret), Huntington Beach, CA

SURVIVAL ON THE SPIRITUAL BATTLEFIELD

A CHRISTIAN WARRIOR TRAINING MANUAL ON HOW TO SAFELY LEAD YOUR FAMILY ON THE BATTLEFIELD AND HOW TO BE VICTORIOUS

SALVADOR (SI) RANGEL

outskirtspress

DENVER, COLORADO

Outskirts Press, Inc.
http://www.outskirtspress.com

ISBN: 978-1-4787-2467-4

Outskirts Press and the "OP" logo are trademarks belonging to Outskirts Press, Inc.

PRINTED IN THE UNITED STATES OF AMERICA

Contents

Dedication

For my wife Chris, her daily encouragement, her devotion to me and her Saviour, her selfless service to the work of the church is an inspiration to me and so many others. To Pastor Bill Rench of Calvary Baptist Church Temecula, CA. without his preaching, teaching, and mentoring this book would not be possible.

To the men of Company C, 3rd Battalion, 12th Special Forces Gp. (Abn), who taught me to soldier.

Acknowledgments

Our first mid-week service at Calvary Baptist church was at Pastor Bill Rench's home in Temecula, CA. There were several families meeting there on Wednesday nights and the Sunday service was at a local elementary school. That first Sunday service we met several church members who became our church family. There were three senior married couples who my wife Chris and I adopted as our spiritual parents: Julius and Marjie Schmitt, Bob and Helen Jordan, Frank and Audry Smalley. These couples also adopted us as their married children and it was under their mentoring as men and women, husbands and wives, as parents, and as serving church members that they encouraged us in our spiritual walk and service to our Lord and Saviour and His church. Chris and I hope we can encourage and mentor younger married couples as well as we were mentored.

Introduction

I retired from the U.S. Army Reserve in 2005 after 41 years of service. I trained for combat for every war and police action the United States has been engaged. In addition to formal doctrinal infantry, intelligence, and special operations training, I received informal training from many decorated infantry combat arms veterans from WWII, Korea, Dominican Republic, Viet Nam, Grenada, Panama, and the first Gulf War. My only combat deployment occurred in 2004 to Afghanistan for one year. I served six months with the Office of Military Cooperation-Afghanistan then transferred to the Combined Joint Special Operations Task Force for another six months. As the saying goes "I was never a hero, but I am thankful and proud to have served among them." As a soldier, I learned not only how to survive on today's lethal battlefield but also how to win on that battlefield.

My goal in writing this book is to share my military education and experience with Christian men and women who are now engaged in spiritual warfare. The tactics used by our common enemy the Taliban and al-Qaida in Afghanistan and Iraq are similar to Satan's tactics on the spiritual battlefield. I want Christians to not only survive on the battlefield but to be victorious as our U.S. military is today. May God bless our military servicemen.

Author's Note

I joined the U.S. Army Reserve as an infantryman on October 28, 1964. I transferred to U.S. Special Forces Reserve in 1967, and then transferred to the California Army National Guard in 1980. I retired from the National Guard as the Command Sergeant Major of the 40th Engineer Brigade in 1996. I re-entered the Army Reserve after 9-11 and retired on my 60th birthday in 2005. In my forty one years of Army Reserve and Army National Guard service I have attended many formal and informal military schools and war games, conferences, training seminars and staff up-dates. As a Sergeant Major my focus has always been mission accomplishment and the welfare of soldiers and their families. I do not consider myself an expert military tactician and the examples I have used are from my own personal experiences and conversations with military veterans with whom I have served.

All Scriptures quoted are from the Authorized King James Bible.

The Battlefield

"Be sober, be vigilant; because your adversary the devil, As a roaring lion, walketh about, seeking whom he may devour."

— 1 Peter 5:8

1 Timothy 1:18 says, "This charge I commit unto thee, son Timothy, according to the prophecies which went before on thee, that thou by them mightest war a good warfare." Paul wrote 1 Timothy around 62-63 AD, a time when Israel was not at war. The warfare Paul was talking about was spiritual warfare as mentioned in Ephesians chapter 6. Verse 12 says, "For we wrestle not against flesh and blood, but against principalities, against powers, against the rulers of the darkness of this world, against spiritual wickedness in high places." The verse refers to a physical contest or hand to hand combat, not against a human foe, but against principalities, powers, rulers of the darkness and spiritual wickedness in high places, which all refer to satanic influence at all levels. This is Spiritual Warfare.

After Satan fell from Heaven he was made the prince of the power of the air (Ephesians 2:2(1)); he has the power to ensnare men and take them captive (2 Timothy 2:26(2)), and he imitates righteous men to deceive others (2 Corinthians 11:13(3)). Peter warns us to beware of Satan in 1 Peter 5:8, "Be sober, be vigilant; because your adversary the devil, as a roaring lion, walketh about seeking whom he may devour." In the book of Job, Satan is asked by God what he has been doing (as if God did not know.) Satan answered in Job 1:7, "... going to and fro in the earth, and from walking up and down in it." Satan is our enemy. He is referred to as the "prince of this world" in John 12:31, "Now is the judgment of this world: now shall the prince of this world be cast out." He owns (4) the entire spiritual battlefield and he knows every square mile of it.

There are two types of warfare; conventional and unconventional. To fully comprehend the lethal unconventional and spiritual battlefield you must understand the conventional battlefield. The best way to explain conventional warfare is for you to remember what you learned about WW 1, WW 2, and the Korean War. There were battle lines drawn. On one side of the line was the U.S. and our allies, and on the other side was the enemy. This line is called by the military the "FEBA" (forward edge of the battle area). There is typically a space of land between our line of soldiers and the enemy soldiers and this is often referred to as "no man's land." Today in Korea this line is called the DMZ or the "demilitarized zone." It is the most dangerous place to be on the battlefield, in between two well- armed, ready opposing forces.

On this conventional battlefield there are three echelons of soldiers. The first echelon are the combat arms soldiers (those who will do the fighting) who are deployed closest to the enemy at the forward edge of the battle area. If the enemy attacks he is attacking you personally. If the enemy is on the defense he is constantly probing your position to see what you are doing. If you are attacking the enemy position you will be in the most dangerous position on the lethal battlefield.

The second echelon are soldiers of "combat tactical support" units. These units provide fire support and tactical operational assistance to combat arms units. They provide specialized support in areas such as chemical warfare, intelligence, security, and communications. These soldiers are positioned to the rear of the combat arms units and are located in well defended positions, but are close enough to the first echelon units so they can provide tactical support in a timely manner. This is the second most dangerous position on the battlefield.

The third echelon are soldiers of "combat service support" units which provide logistical support to combat arms units. These units are composed of supply, maintenance, transportation, and health services. These soldiers are positioned to the rear of combat tactical support units and located in well defended positions. This is the third most dangerous position on the battlefield.

As you can see, the closer a soldier is to the battle line (the forward edge of the battle area) the more danger he is in, and the farther away, the safer he is. Every soldier is aware of the danger and every soldier knows that the enemy is just beyond the battle line.

In conventional warfare the enemy is easily located in a general sense and the enemy is easily identifiable. Just as U.S. soldiers wear distinct battle dress uniforms, the enemy also wears distinct and identifiable combat uniforms. These are agreements made and agreed upon by the Geneva Convention and The Hague /Geneva Protocol and enforced by International Law.

Conventional warfare has been explained simplistically so the danger areas on the battlefield can be easily identified. When our conventional Army is in the "attack" the dangers become significantly increased. As our Army crosses the battle line all of the enemy's echelons of defense (similar to our echelons) are attacked simultaneously by our combat arms units (Infantry, Armor, Field Artillery, Attack Helicopter, Special Forces and Combat Engineer). In the conduct of conventional combat operations special consideration is given to wounded or sick personnel, the treatment of prisoners of war, the protection of civilians, and places of worship, and they are all protected by the Geneva Convention and International law.

In additional to these conventional rules of war the Theatre Commander issues "Rules of Engagement." This standard is used to determine when and where deadly force shall be used. Depending on U.S. policy, or a declared or non-declared war, the rules of engagement vary. As an example the Rules of Engagement for the Somalia Relief Operation is provided as enclosure #1.

Hopefully you now have a basic understanding of Conventional warfare; the forces used, their battle lines, echelons of soldiers and their placement on the battlefield, the rules of engagements, and the danger areas on the battlefield.

Now that you have this knowledge it will be very easy to explain "Unconventional Warfare." First of all, U.S. Forces are organized in the same configuration and echelons of soldiers in both conventional and unconventional warfare. Second, and a big second, there are NO battle lines. Third, the enemy has no standard uniform (he typically wears civilian clothing). Fourth, the Geneva/Hague convention, the Laws of Warfare and rules of engagement apply to U.S. forces, but not the enemy. Fifth and last, there are no rules for the enemy.

The objective of unconventional warfare is to induce war weariness on the opposing force and their country, the curtailment of civilian standards of living in the battle area, economic hardship linked to the costs of war, a helplessness to defend against assaults, fear, depression, and the disintegration of morale. The ultimate goal of unconventional warfare is to motivate the enemy to stop attacking or resisting even when he has the ability to continue. And this is what Spiritual Warfare is all about.

Paul warned us about spiritual warfare and identified the enemy for us in Ephesians 6:12 which says, "For we wrestle not against flesh and blood, but against principalities, against powers, against the rulers of the darkness of this world, against spiritual wickedness in high places." The word "principalities" in the verse refers to a government who has declared war against Christianity. As example when government orders the Ten Commandments (5) off government buildings and court rooms, by taking prayer and the Bible out of the public classroom, by embracing evolution and teaching it as fact, by redefining the family, and teaching tolerance to "alternate lifestyles" all of which the Bible calls "sin."

Spiritual warfare is also against "powers" or invisible beings who have dominion over parts of creation, such as the one Paul warns us about in this verse who is identified as the "ruler of the darkness of this world." Spiritual warfare is also against those in "high places" who have influence over government at City, County, State, or National level. It could even be your local public school board officials who teach youths their rights as adults, who counsel female students to abort their pregnancies, who teach the theory of evolution as fact, who teach your children to be tolerant of sin. This is Spiritual Warfare.

If you're a born again believer, if you're saved, if you have invited Jesus Christ into your heart as your Lord and Saviour, then you are not only in the family of God (Romans 8:15(6)) but are also in God's Army. As a Christian soldier you are the one who fights the spiritual battle against Satan. You are the infantry soldier that Satan attacks. Since he can never defeat our Lord and Saviour, he looks for followers and disciples of Christ to war against. Scripture commands the Christian to "Be sober, be vigilant: because your adversary the devil, as a roaring lion, walketh about, seeking whom he may devour" 1 Peter 5:8. The words sober and vigilant are military terms for a soldier on guard duty. Sober means to be serious and solemn, and vigilant means to be watchful and attentive to discover and avoid danger or to provide for the safety of yourself and fellow soldiers. The verse tells the Christian who the adversary, or enemy is: the devil. And that he is walking around the earth seeking his enemy to devour, destroy, annihilate or consume him. When Satan was thrown from heaven he took 1/3 of the angels with him and these are his entire army. Revelation 12:9 says, "And the great dragon was cast out, that old serpent, called the Devil, and Satan, which deceiveth the whole world: he was cast out into the earth, and his angels were cast out with him." This is why Christians have daily battles on the spiritual battlefield that we live in.

The Christian soldier must be strong and courageous on the battlefield to survive and to be victorious. The Bible has numerous verses for the Christian soldier; 1 Corinthians 16:13(7) and 2 Timothy 2:1(8) warn to watch, stand fast and to be strong; 1 Kings 2:2(9), Isaiah 35:4(10) and 2 Chronicles 15:7(11) say to be strong, manly and to fear not. And Joshua told the nation Israel before entering the Promised Land in 10:25 "…fear not, nor be dismayed, be strong and of good courage: for thus shall the Lord do to all your enemies against whom ye fight."

The U.S. soldier today is almost always outnumbered on the battle-field. The U.S. military relies on high tech weapons systems and rugged advanced individual training of the soldier to overcome the enemy. Today's soldier has at his disposal a Quick Reaction Force for immediate reinforcement when needed, he also has heavy artillery, helicopter gun ships, air support, cruise missiles, etc. Today's soldier enters the battlefield confident, courageous, and fearless. That is why the Taliban and al-Qaida will only challenge the U.S. military on the unconventional battlefield where he can easily hide and escape amongst the civilian population.

The Christian soldier on the spiritual battlefield should be just as confident, courageous, and fearless as the U.S. soldier. God has promised His protection to every believer. In 2 Kings chapter 6 the prophet Elisha and his servant were surrounded by chariots of the Syrian kings army. The servant was fearful and Elisha told him in verse 16 "…Fear not: for they that be with us are more than they that be with them." So the servant not believing what he could not see was prayed for by Elisha in verse 17 for God to open his eyes "And Elisha prayed, and said, Lord, I pray thee, open his eyes, that he may see. And the Lord opened the eyes of the young man; and he saw: and, behold, the mountain was full of horses and chariots of fire round about Elisha."

Every Christian soldier has Divine protection on the spiritual battlefield. Exodus 14:14(12) and 23:27(13) tell us the Lord will fight for you, and He will make our enemies turn their backs to us; 2 Chronicles 20:29(14) and 32:8(15) tell us that the Lord will fight against our enemies and fight our battles. King David refers to God as his protector, his buckler, his shield, his deliverer, his refuge, his rock, his fortress, his high tower and in Psalm 18:3 he says "I will call upon the Lord, who is worthy to be praised: so shall I be saved from mine enemies." God still saves his children from their enemies. Luke 10:19 says "Behold, I give unto you power to tread on serpents and scorpions, and over all the power of the enemy: and nothing shall by any means hurt you."

The soldier on the unconventional battlefield is in danger 24/7. There are no battle lines. The enemy is all around, he has no standard uniform or weapon, and there are no safe areas. The Christian soldier on the spiritual battlefield is in just as much danger. To survive and be victorious he must be just as well trained as the infantry soldier.

The Enemy

"The enemy said, I will pursue, I will overtake, I will divide the spoil; my lust shall be satisfied upon them; I will draw my sword, my hand shall destroy them."

– Exodus 15:9

In order for a soldier and his unit to survive and be victorious on the battlefield, he must know all there is to know about the enemy. In the military this knowledge is referred to as intelligence. Intelligence is knowledge acquired by the collection, evaluation, analysis, integration, and interpretation of all available information concerning a possible or actual enemy or areas of operations, including weather and terrain. Enemy intelligence includes their probable course of action which can affect mission accomplishment.

There are two types of enemy intelligence, Strategic and Combat. Strategic intelligence pertains to the capabilities, vulnerabilities, and probable courses of action of foreign nations. This includes information on the countries' entire military services and the countries' war making abilities. It is produced primarily for the use of high level military commanders charged with the planning and execution of national security measures in time of peace and with the conduct of military operations in a time of war. Combat intelligence is for use in a combat situation that is collected locally or provided by higher headquarters. Combat intelligence has two objectives: First, to reduce to a minimum all uncertainties regarding the enemy, weather, and terrain, and thus to assist the commander in making a decision and the troops in executing their mission. Second, to assist the commander in applying counterintelligence and security measures that will conceal from the enemy the intentions and activities and will neutralize or destroy the effectiveness of enemy intelligence activities.

The infantryman who is fighting the day to day battle is only interested in combat intelligence and how it affects him, his unit, their survival and mission accomplishment. The intelligence product that is most beneficial is the enemy order of battle. The order of battle is what the infantryman can expect to encounter while deployed on the battlefield. This intelligence information is derived by the assessment of the following factors of the enemy:

- Composition: This identifies the command structure and organization of enemy units. Such as: is the enemy infantry, armor, artillery, engineer etc., or what attachments or detachments does he have.

- Disposition: Where are the locations of his headquarters and units and how are they deployed.

- Strength: The numerical strength and the weight of fire that can be delivered by his weapons systems.

- Tactics: How he employs his forces on the battlefield.

- Training: This refers to specialized training of the basic enemy unit. The enemy unit may be infantry but it may also be Airborne infantry with mountain warfare and cold weather training.

- Logistics: How and in what amount does the enemy obtain its supplies?

- Units: The unit combat history can be used to judge expected performance.

- Personalities: Known enemy personnel and their past behavior.

- Morale: What is the physical, mental and emotional condition of the unit?

- Capabilities and limitations: What is the enemy's most likely course of action? Will he defend, reinforce, attack, withdraw, or delay?

As you can see the more information or intelligence a soldier has about his enemy he is that much more likely to be able to not only survive on the lethal battlefield but he will be victorious. These same intelligence factors apply just as favorably to the Christian warrior on today's spiritual battlefield.

Let us research scripturally our enemy, Satan, his army, and their order of battle. First of all Satan is an angel. The existence of angels is confirmed 108 times in the Old Testament and 165 times in the New Testament. They were created at the time of God's creative acts as recorded in the book of Genesis. They are personal beings and possess the attributes of personality. They are powerful but not omnipotent. They were created with a holy nature, though not with a holy character. Like man they have the freedom to obey or disobey. 2 Peter 2:4 says, "For if God spared not the angels that sinned, but cast them down to hell, and delivered them into chains of darkness, to be reserved unto judgment."

Satan was the first fallen angel and he led other angels in a rebellion. Isaiah 14:13-14 describes his fall as a result of pride, "For thou hast said in thine heart, I will ascend into heaven, I will exalt my throne above the stars of God: I will sit also upon the mount of the congregation, in the sides of the north: I will ascend above the heights of the clouds; I will be like the most High." As a result, he was cast out of heaven as described in Rev 12:9, "And the great dragon was cast out, that old serpent, called the Devil, and Satan, which deceiveth the whole world: he was cast out into the earth, and his angels were cast out with him." The Bible does not say how many angels fell and were cast out with Satan, but we may assume he has a large army of them.

The Bible has a lot to say about Satan and describes his character for us in some detail. Just as it is helpful to learn of the personality of the enemy commander it is helpful for the Christian warrior to learn about the personality of the enemy commander on the spiritual battlefield. First of all, he is prideful as we learned in Isaiah 14:13-14. Second, he is wicked, promotes sin, is treacherous and ensnares men. 2 Timothy 2:26 says, "And that they may recover themselves out of the snare of the devil, who are taken captive by him at his will." Satan and his army of angels imitate righteousness as stated in 2 Corinthians 11:14-15, "And no marvel; for Satan himself is transformed into an angel of light. Therefore it is no great thing if his ministers also be transformed as the ministers of righteousness; whose end shall be according to their works."

Satan is opposed to anything good or of God and seeks allegiance from all God's creation. 1 Peter 5:8 refers to him as our adversary. He works among unsaved men and women who are his children. Acts 13:10 says "And said, O full of all subtilty and all mischief, thou child of the devil, thou enemy of all righteousness, wilt thou not cease to pervert the right ways of the Lord?" The unsaved may be possessed by Satan and they are blinded and easily deceived by him as stated in 2 Corinthians 4:4(1). Satan works among Believers by tempting them and he accuses and deceives Christians as stated in Revelation 12:9(2). His tactics are discussed in greater detail in a latter chapter.

The Bible also teaches of the existence of beings known as devils, demons, evil and wicked spirits in reference to fallen angels both in the Old and New Testaments. These beings have been recognized by Jesus Christ in Mark 16:17(3), by the Lord's church in Luke 10:17(4), and in 1 Corinthians 10:21(5). These devils, demons and evil spirits are all fallen angels who made the choice of following Satan. They are all intelligent in that they know who Jesus is. In the book of Mark chapter 5, as an example, Jesus commands an evil spirit to come out of a man who he had possession of. Verse 7 and 8 says, "And cried with a loud voice, and said, What have I to do with thee Jesus, thou Son of the most high God? I adjure thee by God, that thou torment me not. For he said unto him, Come out of the man, thou unclean spirit." In the next verse Jesus asked the spirit his name and he answered in verse 9, "…my name is Legion: for we are many." In biblical times a Roman army "Legion" consisted of three to five thousand infantry soldiers.

These fallen angels are vicious, vile, and malicious. They cause personal injury in Mark 9:18(6), blindness in Matthew 12:22(7), deformities in Luke 13:11(8), insanity in Luke 8:26-36(9), and suicide in Mark 9:22(10). These devils attempt to cause spiritual perversion by the rise of false doctrines and cults as stated in 1 Timothy 4:1-3, "Now the Spirit speaketh expressly, that in the latter times some shall depart from the faith, giving heed to seducing spirits, and doctrines of devils: Speaking lies in hypocrisy; having their conscience seared with a hot iron; Forbidding to marry, and commanding to abstain from meats, which God hath created to be received with thanksgiving of them which believe and know the truth."

Satan and evil spirits are powerful, but they also have limitations. As created beings they are not omniscient, omnipotent nor omnipresent. They only know what they can see and hear themselves, where God, Jesus Christ, and the Holy Spirit are all knowing, all powerful and are everywhere present. An example of their limitations is found in the book of Job chapter one. The chapter says there was a day when

Satan came before the Lord and He asked Satan where he had been (as if He didn't know). Satan answered in verse 7, "… From going to and fro in the earth, and from walking up and down in it." (Satan's character shows that his travels on earth are for evil purposes. 1 Peter 5:8 describes Satan as "…your adversary the devil…seeking whom he may devour.") In the next verse God asked Satan if he had considered Job who is "… a perfect and upright man, one that feareth God, and escheweth evil?" In the next few verses Satan explains Job is "upright" only because God has blessed him physically, financially, and spiritually, and placed a "hedge" of protection around him, but if God took it all away Job would "…curse thee to thy face." And in verse 12 God gives Satan limited powers by saying "…Behold, all that he hath is in thy power; only upon himself put not forth thine hand. So Satan went forth from the presence of the Lord."

Just as God protected Job in the Old Testament every Christian is protected in the same manner today on the spiritual battlefield. The "hedge" reveals all that God does to protect His children. Satan's power is always under the control of God. Consequently his "morale" is low. Satan is already a defeated enemy. The Bible says Jesus Christ destroyed the works of Satan in 1 John 3:8 "He that committeth sin is of the devil; for the devil sinneth from the beginning. For this purpose the Son of God was manifested, that he might destroy the works of the devil." Satan, because of his coming destruction, is desperate. He still seeks to be God and steal the hearts of men.

These few chapters give only a glimpse of Satan and his devils' "order of battle." Just as the infantry soldier will never underestimate his foe the Christian warrior on the spiritual battlefield should never underestimate Satan in the daily battle.

The Soldier and His Training

"Thou therefore endure hardness, as a good soldier of Jesus Christ."

– 2 Timothy 2:3

When Paul told Timothy to "war a good warfare" in 1 Timothy 1:18 he was giving him a "charge" (…This charge I commit unto thee, son Timothy…) as a preacher and as a soldier. To "charge" means to lay on as a duty, order, or command; to enjoin or exhort to accomplish a duty. The nation Israel was not at war when Paul gave this charge to Timothy. He was referring to spiritual warfare. This "charge" to Timothy is also for every Christian today. The "charge" is just as important today as it was when given to Timothy. So the question is how did Timothy "war a good warfare" and how can we war a good warfare on today's spiritual battlefield?

Both conventional and unconventional warfare really has not changed much over the centuries. The "principles of war" first defined by Sun Tzu around 500 BC is still taught today at the Military Academies all over the world. The men change, their uniforms change, weapons change, transportation methods change, but the principles of war are the same. To be victorious on today's lethal battlefield a soldier must be able to survive on the battlefield and he must be able to accomplish his mission. So first let us focus on the soldier and his survival on the battlefield.

When a civilian joins the Army he immediately begins Basic Training or Boot Camp. In the Army, Basic Training is eight weeks long and focuses on two subjects: the transformation of a civilian into a soldier and his survival on the battlefield. If you served in the military you remember Basic Training and if you did not serve you probably have a relative, friend, or neighbor who did. When they returned home after Basic Training they were different they were not the same person who left physically or mentally. They were what the Bible calls "transformed" no longer a civilian but now a Soldier. Romans 12:2 says, "And be not conformed to this world: but be ye transformed by the renewing of your mind, that ye may prove what is that good, and acceptable, and perfect, will of God."

How did this transformation take place, from private citizen to Army Private? You do not become a soldier by a correspondence course, Army on-line course, computer games, or watching reality TV, but by eight weeks of intensive individual training and hard work. It's a total 24/7 immersion training program. After getting a short hair cut, a uniform, boots and immunizations the recruit is introduced to his Drill Instructor called a "DI." The DI is the first person the recruit sees every morning before dawn and the last person he sees before he collapses at the end of the day. The DI has one hundred per cent of the civilian's attention. In Basic Training there are no outside influences. No television, no newspapers, no music, no old friends, no parents, no relatives, no telephone, no computers, no game boys, no parties, no car, no bars, no alcohol, no drugs, no clothing fashions, and no restaurants. There is nothing that will divert the recruit's attention from the DI. The DI takes the recruit all the way through the eight weeks of training. He teaches him how to live in a barracks with forty other soldiers, how to wear his uniform, how to march; he teaches military terminology, and gets him into physical condition to do battle. The recruit is issued a weapon, learns its characteristics, how to disassemble and assemble, and immediate action for a malfunction, then undergoes bayonet training, and must qualify at the rifle range. The DI teaches the three General Orders of guard duty, how to follow orders, and how to be a team member. The recruit learns the Army Core Values of loyalty, duty, respect, selfless service, honor, integrity and personal courage.

The Army recruit must be healthy, strong, and physically fit so he is able to meet every challenge on the battlefield. So diet and exercise during training is important. Every meal the new soldier is given has been measured by nutritionists to ensure that he has a proper diet to build muscle and endurance. Have you noticed the physical changes in the young men and women who have returned home after successfully graduating from Basic Training? It is a result of a proper diet and a strenuous physical fitness program.

Survival on the battlefield takes physical endurance. One day on the battlefield can seem as a month. Therefore, every phase of infantry training for the soldier involves daily calisthenics and running. The Army physical fitness test is conducted monthly to record a soldier's improvement. The physical events of the test measure a soldier's physical endurance. Survival on the battlefield is not a sprint, it is running a marathon. The apostle Paul warns the Christian soldier of the necessity of endurance when he says in Hebrews 12:1, "…let us lay aside every weight, and the sin which doth so easily beset us, and let us run with patience the race that is set before us." Christians have to run with patience because spiritual warfare is a prolonged war, just as it was in Iraq and is currently in Afghanistan. Paul warns that there are many hazards, many danger areas and many obstacles for the Christian as he describes events in his life in 2 Corinthians 11:24-28 which says, "Of the Jews five times received I forty stripes save one. Thrice was I beaten with rods, once was I stoned, thrice I suffered shipwreck, a night and a day I have been in the deep; In journeying often, in perils of water, in perils of robbers, in perils by mine own countrymen, in perils by the heathen, in perils in the city, in perils in the wilderness, in perils in the sea, in perils among false brethren; In weariness and painfulness, in watchings often, in hunger and thirst, in fastings often, in cold and nakedness. Beside those things that are without, that which cometh upon me daily, the care of all the churches."

The Christian soldier must also have the proper diet and exercise to meet the challenges on the spiritual battlefield. Scripture often refers to the word of God as food for the Christian. Psalm 119:103 says, "How sweet are thy words unto my taste! Yea, sweeter than honey to my mouth" and Job 23:12 says, "…I have esteemed the words of his mouth more than my necessary food." Scripture refers to the prolonged spiritual battle physically as running a race. And 1 Corinthians chapter nine teaches the importance of running and physical fitness. Verse 24 says, "Know ye not that they which run in a race run all, but one receiveth the prize? So run, that ye may obtain." The next verse 25 teaches every Christian soldier to be "temperate in all things" and in verses 26 and 27 Paul says he runs "not as uncertainly; so fight I, not as one that beateth the air: But I keep under my body and bring it into subjection…" In these few verses the Apostle Paul is teaching the importance of the self-discipline of the body of the believer to avert being disqualified as a soldier on the spiritual battlefield and Christian service.

The soldier on the battlefield eats MRE's (Meal Ready to Eat). Each individual meal contains approximately 1,200 calories when the entire meal is consumed and sustains the soldier during combat operations. Likewise the Bible is able to sustain the Christian soldier on the spiritual battlefield but he must consume its contents on a consistent and daily basis.

Every soldier remembers his Drill Instructor and wants to be just as professional as he was. The DI was his father figure and older brother;

he received discipline from him when things went wrong and praise from him when things went according to plan. The DI was his personal trainer and mentor. Eight weeks of Basic Training is what it takes to transform a civilian recruit into a soldier who can survive on today's lethal battlefield.

Just as every soldier has to be taught how to "soldier," every new Christian has to be taught how to become a follower and disciple of Jesus Christ. Just as every soldier needs a mentor or Drill Instructor to teach him soldiering skills, how to become a team player and become unified with his unit members, the new Christian learns how to be in accord with all church members. Just as every soldier takes off his civilian clothing and the DI teaches him how to wear and respect the uniform, every new Christian needs a mentor to teach him how to dress modestly. Just as every soldier learns to march and learns Army terminology the new Christian learns how to behave and speak as a Christian and how to serve his Lord and Saviour.

The new Christian should undergo the same training philosophy as the soldier. He has to transform himself from the sinner he was into a soldier in God's Army. He does this by the renewing of his mind by reading the Word of God and the teaching and preaching of the Word of God. 2 Timothy 2:15 says, "Study to shew thyself approved unto God, a workman that needeth not to be ashamed, rightly dividing the word of truth." This is why Paul told Timothy how to become a soldier for Christ in 2 Timothy 2:4, "No man that warreth entangleth himself with the affairs of this life; that he may please him who hath chosen him to be a soldier." God chooses his soldiers from hand picked volunteers who repent of their sins. Christians are not drafted into his service, but are adopted into His army. Ephesians 1:5 says, "Having predestinated us unto the adoption of children by Jesus Christ to himself, according to the good pleasure of his will," and just as new soldiers are separated from civilians and enter into Basic Training the new Christian has to separate himself from the "affairs of this life." 1 Peter 1:14-15 says, "As obedient children, not fashioning, yourselves according to the former lusts in your ignorance: But as he which hath called you is holy, so be ye holy in all manner of conversation." Christians are not to be concerned with the latest fads, trends, or the oldest traditions. We are to separate ourselves from our former lusts, from all our former influences so we can focus on the Word of God and the Holy Spirit within us. Just as the civilian becomes a new soldier, the saved sinner becomes a new Christian. 2 Corinthians 5:17 says, "Therefore if any man be in Christ, he is a new creature: old things are passed away; behold, all things are become new."

Every new Christian should go through a one-on-one Discipleship Training program. This training is much like a soldier's Basic Training. Without this initial training, the new Christian will not survive on the spiritual battlefield. He will become an easy (soft) target of the enemy and will become KIA (Killed In Action), WIA (Wounded In Action) or MIA (Missing In Action). Hebrews 5:12-13 says, "For when for the time ye ought to be teachers, ye have need that one teach you again which be the first principles of the oracles of God; and are become such as have need of milk, and not of strong meat. For every one that useth milk is unskillful in the word of righteousness: for he is a babe."

Discipleship training is not only for the new Christian, it is also good refresher training for the mature Christian, or for the Christian who over the years has not had the opportunity to attend in-depth local church Bible studies. The two-fold purpose of Discipleship training is to provide the Christian with the Biblical fundamentals so he can become well grounded in the truth of the Word of God; and secondly so he will be able to recognize untruth when he hears it taught or preached. Remember 2 Timothy 2:15 says, "Study to shew thyself approved unto God..."

Like the recruit who needs his Drill Instructor, the new Christian needs a mentor or discipler to help explain the Scriptures and how to apply these practical Biblical truths into their every day lives. When a new Christian does not become well grounded in Biblical truths he is easy prey for the false religions, false teachers, and false preachers. 2 Peter 2:1 says, "But there were false prophets also among the people, even as there shall be false teachers among you…" If you're a new Christian, or a Christian who has not completed a local church Discipleship training program you must get into one today. There is an example of Discipleship subjects in enclosure #2.

Discipleship training usually begins explaining the organization, canonization, and preservation of the Holy Bible; explains salvation and how man is delivered from condemnation to have eternal life with and through Jesus Christ; provides Biblical assurance of salvation; studies the Godhead of the Father, His son Jesus Christ, and the Holy Spirit; studies the New Testament church, its importance, purpose, organization, and leadership; studies why, how, when and the hindrances of prayer; explains how to have a close personal relationship with Jesus Christ; and how to witness and lead someone to Christ. And last it should introduce the new Christian to the Biblical doctrines of man, sin, angels, and of end times.

Just as the completion of Basic Training provides the new recruit the ability and confidence to survive on the battlefield, Discipleship training gives the new Christian the same ability and confidence to survive on the spiritual battlefield. As Basic Training transforms the life of a civilian to the life of a soldier, Discipleship training transforms the life of a sinner into the life of a Christian warrior.

The second phase of Army Training is your specialty training or MOS (Military Occupational Specialty). Remember, Basic Training transforms the civilian into a soldier and teaches how to survive on the battlefield. Specialty training teaches the soldier his specific job in the military. A soldier without advanced specialty training can survive on the battlefield but, for what purpose? With specialty training he can perform his specific duty as a squad or team member and the squad can accomplish their mission. As an example, a soldier could be in the infantry, military police, artillery, medical, communications, transportations, etc. This specialty training can last anywhere from six weeks to two and ½ years depending on the schooling required to become MOS qualified.

Specialty training is more important than the eight week Basic Training course. Yes, with Basic Training you will be able to survive on the battlefield, but after the completion of your specialty training you have a purpose for being on the battlefield. As a trained soldier you will be given a mission on a field of battle and the responsibility to accomplish the mission assigned to you by your commander.

An Army is comprised of many Branches of service and each Branch has several MOS specialties. For example, the branch's include Infantry, Armor, Cavalry, Field Artillery, Combat Engineer, Combat Aviation, etc. All branches and individual specialties work together. When each branch accomplishes their mission it allows the Army to accomplish its overall combat mission on the conventional or unconventional battlefield. If, for example, the Chemical Branch did not accomplish their mission it could jeopardize the mission of the entire Army. Every Branch, every specialty, every soldier must be able to not only survive but must be able to accomplish their mission on the battlefield.

After successful completion of MOS specialty training the soldier is assigned to a Army "unit" that needs his skills. A unit that does not have all of its soldiers properly trained and qualified is not deployable to a Theatre of war. Each soldier is unique in his specialty and once assigned to a unit with other equally trained soldiers the unit becomes mission capable, deployable, morale improves, and the unit develops cohesiveness with soldiers caring for one another.

Throughout all training of the recruit teamwork is emphasized.

Beginning at Basic Training the soldier has a "buddy" to team up with. They help each other throughout all phases of Basic Training. Teamwork then builds as the soldier continues his specialty training. Soldiers learn the importance of teamwork, and as their training continues they learn to rely on all team members for survivability on the battlefield, for mutual support, and for mission accomplishment.

A Christian who is not a local church member is like an untrained soldier on the battlefield without a unit. He may be surviving but he has no commander and no direction. He may be finding things to keep himself busy but there is no overall objective, purpose or mission. A lone soldier cannot function well. He spends his time with tasks and duties for his survival but does not function in his specialty and he may never do so. A lone Christian is AWOL (absent without leave) from the local church.

The local church to a Christian is the same as an Army unit to a soldier. The church is the Christian's Army headquarters. The church is where he receives his training, his orders, his security and care. As he matures in Christian growth he trains and mentors other new Christians. It is the church who provides him objectives, purpose, a mission and deploys him into the mission field.

Some Christians today say the church is not important anymore. They say they can read the Bible themselves and have fellowship with home Bible studies, and serve God outside the institution of the local church. Others are just too lazy to get up on Sunday mornings to attend church so they watch a service on television or listen to a service on the radio. Of all the television and radio personalities, most are not preachers and they give sermons to an audience, not a church congregation. These so called minister personalities are interested in their ratings, not the message, and there is no personal contact between the viewer/listener and the personality.

Preaching the Gospel of Jesus Christ, and preaching the Word of God in the house of God is a life saving proposition for the Preacher. The importance of Jesus Christ dying and shedding his blood on the cross of Calvary for the sinner can never be overemphasized. Jesus Christ sacrificed his life for the sinner and soldiers sacrifice their lives not only for their comrades in arms but also for the citizens at home. Soldiers in war sometimes give their lives in the defense of their comrades. As an example, Michael A. Monsoor, Petty Officer Second Class, member of SEAL Team 3 on 29 September 2006, while in an intense firefight on a roof top in Ar Ramadi, Iraq, was struck by a hand grenade from an unseen location. The grenade bounced off Monsoor's chest and landed in front of him. Although only he could have escaped the blast, Petty Officer Monsoor chose instead to protect his teammates. Instantly and without regard for his own safety, he threw himself onto the grenade to absorb the force of the explosion with his body, saving the lives of his teammates. As a result he received the Medal of Honor.

Soldiers and civilians are willing to give their lives for people they love, whether it is a fellow soldier, family member or other loved one, because that person is important to them. This is the same reason Jesus Christ died on the Cross for every sinner and the church. Ephesians 5:25 says, "…Christ also loved the church and gave himself for it." And Acts 20:28 says, "Take heed therefore unto your selves, and to all the flock, over the which the Holy Ghost hath made you overseers, to feed the church of God, which he hath purchased with his own blood." Christ willingly died and shed His blood on Calvary's cross for the church. If the church was this important to Jesus Christ, then the church is important for every Christian warrior to attend.

An Army is not just a General, his entourage and his marching band. An Army is ready-trained soldiers assembled together to accomplish every mission given by their commander so they, working and soldiering together, can win the land battle. The local church is similar. Church is not just a building. It is an assembly of baptized believers gathered together to worship God, praise God, and to accomplish his work.

Military formations are important and attendance is mandatory by every soldier. A formation is when all members of a unit assemble together in ordered ranks and roll is called to account for each and every soldier. Information is then given on the day's operations, the enemy and their intentions, and how it affects the unit's mission. A soldier who misses a formation in a time of war is subject to disciplinary action. This action can result in anything from a reduction in rank to the death penalty.

Every single soldier on the battlefield is important. He is a team member and is vital for mission accomplishment. An infantry squad or team missing even one member cannot function nor operate as it should and may compromise mission accomplishment. As an example let's examine how an infantry squad (10 men) executes an "L" shaped ambush. Let's begin by defining an ambush: It is a surprise attack from a concealed position on a moving or temporarily halted target. The key planning considerations for the squad leader are: Covering the entire kill zone by fire, using existing or reinforcing obstacles to keep the enemy in the kill zone, protecting the assault and support elements with mines, using security elements or teams to isolate the kill zone, assaulting into the kill zone to search dead and wounded, assembling prisoners, collecting equipment, and timing the actions of all elements of the squad to preclude loss of surprise.

In a squad size ambush of this type the squad is divided into three elements: command and control, support, and assault. The assault element forms the long leg parallel to the enemy's direction of movement along the kill zone. The support element forms the short leg at one end of and at right angles to the assault element. This technique provides both flanking and enfilading fires against the enemy. The L-shaped ambush is best used at a sharp bend in a trail, road, or stream. In addition to the three elements of the ambush formation each squad member will have additional duties. Such as an enemy prisoner of war (EPW) search team member, demolition team of enemy vehicles and/ or equipment, flank security team, or a first aid/litter team member.

Once the ambush has been initiated the security teams provide flank and rear security while the assault team enters the kill zone. This team then collects, secures and searches all enemy prisoners of war, identifies and collects enemy equipment, prepares it for transport, and collects the remaining enemy equipment for destruction. While this is being completed the first aid/litter team is treating friendly wounded.

As you can see a simple "L" shaped ambush conducted by a ten man infantry squad has many individual critical tasks that have to be accomplished by every member of the squad. Each squad and team member has to know his particular task, when to attempt it, and how to complete it for the mission to be successful. If one member is missing from the squad another member must be assigned to his tasks or the mission will be compromised.

It is the same for the New Testament church. Every church member has a duty, has a mission, and is important for the overall success of the local church on the spiritual battlefield. Just as the infantry is composed of individual soldiers from all walks of life and from every corner of America who come together to form an infantry squad, the church is composed of individuals in the same way to form a church. Just as every military service member takes an oath of enlistment, the Christian soldier also takes an oath.

An oath is a vow or promise and is used in Scripture frequently. As an example Numbers 30:2 says, "If a man vow a vow unto the Lord, or swear an oath to bind his soul with a bond; he shall not break his word, he shall do according to all that proceeded out of his mouth." Upon salvation the Christian binds himself to the Word of God; it becomes his manual for life and is considered his oath. It contains his "words" to live by. 2 Timothy 3:16 says, "All scripture is given by inspiration of God, and is profitable for doctrine (what is right), for reproof (what is not right), for correction (how to make wrongs right) and instruction in righteousness (how to stay right)."

As a soldier joins the military and becomes part of a team the new Christian soldier joins the New Testament local church and becomes part of a team. The church member is ordered in James 1:22, "But be ye doers of the word, and not hearers only…" and verse 25 orders, "… being not a forgetful hearer, but a doer of the work…" Ephesians 4: 11-12 teaches that God gave each church specific workers and how they should be used, "And he gave some, apostles; and some, prophets; and some evangelists; and some, pastors and teachers; For the perfecting of the saints, for the work of the ministry, for the edifying of the body of Christ." The apostles, prophets, evangelists, pastors, and teachers are to be used for the perfecting of the saints which refers to training and equipping the church members; the work of the ministry refers to Christian service; and edifying the body of Christ refers to the building up of the church numerically and spiritually. Ephesians 4:16 refers to the entire church body who should all come and work together when it says, "From whom the whole body fitly joined together and compacted by that which every joint supplieth, according to the effectual work-ing in the measure of every part, maketh increase of the body unto the edifying of itself in love." These verses teach that it is Christ who unites the Christian warriors to Himself and brings the church body into a relationship with one another as they perform Christian ministries.

Just as it takes every infantry squad member to successfully employ an "L" shaped ambush it also takes every church member to accomplish and perform Christian service. If one team member is AWOL (absent without leave), MIA or WIA the ambush may be unsuccessful. This is just as important for every church member and it is why Ephesians 4:16 teaches that church members are part of a church body and that they are "fitly joined together" to complete the squad or team.

As you can see, every individual soldier doing his duty is important for success on the battlefield. It is the same for every individual Christian in the local church. Every time the church doors are open should be considered a "formation." Just as the soldier receives new information about daily activities, intelligence about the enemy situation, what Army units are doing on his right and left and new missions the commander has for him; the Christian receives similar information from the preacher. The unit commander receives his informational and intelligence briefing update from many sources. However, not all sources are reliable and have to be confirmed by multiple intelligence agencies and adjacent Army units. For the Christian in church all information is current, trustworthy, and pertains to his area of operation on the battlefield.

The Christian can rely one hundred percent on his sources of information and they do not have to be confirmed. The pastor of the local church receives his information from the most reliable source on heaven and earth, the Bible and the Holy Spirit. The King James Bible is not just a book. It is sixty- six books authored by the Holy Ghost and penned by holy men of God. 2 Peter 1:20-21 says, "Knowing this first, that no prophecy of the scripture is of any private interpretation. For the prophecy came not in old time by the will of man: but holy men of God spake as they were moved by the Holy Ghost." Every single word in the King James Bible is important and has meaning. That is why men are warned not to add or subtract words because it is perfect the way it was written. Deuteronomy 4:2 says, "Ye shall not add unto the word which I command you, neither shall ye diminish ought from it, that ye may keep the commandments of the Lord your God which I command you." The Bible contains life-giving truth and is as important today as it was when written. 2 Timothy 3:16-17 says, "All scripture is given by inspiration of God, and is profitable for doctrine, for reproof, for correction, for instruction in righteousness: That the man of God may be perfect, throughly furnished unto all good works." The King James Bible is the inspired, inerrant, infallible, preserved word of God. Every soldier and Christian can bet their lives that every word is true.

The preacher of the local New Testament church prepares every message from the Word of God, asking help and guidance from the Spirit of God. The message needs no verification or confirmation. As the preacher studies the Word of God and prays, the Holy Spirit delivers His message just as he did in chapter two and three of the book of Revelation. In these chapters God has a unique message to each of the seven churches. Each message is delivered by the angel of the church and in the context of these two chapters the word "angel" is defined as "messenger" or "preacher." The messenger or angel of each local church is the preacher who delivers the message. God knows the pastor of each church, He knows the people of each church, He knows the works of each church, He knows the needs of each church, and He knows the spiritual, economic, and physical condition of each church and its members. There is not just one generic message for all seven churches; there are seven different messages to seven different pastors or angels because each church is unique. God delivers his message the same way today to every Christian. If you missed church, then you missed a formation that delivered important life-saving information for you, your comrades and your family.

The local church pastor is not giving a sermon to a television or radio audience. He is preaching to his friends, his flock, and his church family. He knows every church member personally and they know him personally. He knows what church members are exposed to in their neighborhood, he knows what is going on in each church family, he knows who is out of work and who is sick, he knows the fashions, trends, and traditions of the area because he lives in the same town. He knows what "word" the church needs to hear every Sunday morning. Just as the military commander is responsible for the health, welfare, and training of his men, the local preacher has the same duty and responsibility for his congregation.

The Bible uses three titles for the one office of pastor, they are bishop, elder and pastor. The titles are used interchangeably for the same office but provide three different responsibilities of the pastor. The title Pastor describes the office of under shepherd. The Chief Shepherd is

Jesus Christ. 1 Peter 5:4 is referring to Jesus Christ when it says, "And when the chief Shepherd shall appear, ye shall receive a crown of glory that fadeth not away." The title Bishop describes the duty of the office as an overseer and the title Elder describes the dignity of the office as ruler.

Unlike a military commander, a pastor is a gift to the local church from God. The book of Acts 13:2 gives us an example of the "calling" for every pastor in the New Testament church "As they ministered to the Lord, and fasted, the Holy Ghost said, Separate me Barnabas and Saul for the work whereunto I have called them." A pastor then becomes God's caretaker or overseer of church membership. 1 Peter 2:25 says, "For ye were as sheep going astray; but are now returned unto the Shepherd and Bishop of your souls."

A Pastor is responsible to lead, feed, and heed the flock. Leading is the duty of an Elder who must exercise God-given authority. 1 Thessalonians 5:12 says, "And we beseech you, brethren, to know them which labour among you, and are over you in the Lord, and admonish you." And Hebrews 13:7 says, "Remember them which have rule over you, who have spoken unto you the word of God: whose faith follow…" Just as the best military commanders lead by example, church members are told to follow the examples of their leadership in 1 Peter 5:3, "Neither as being lords over God's heritage, but being examples to the flock."

A Shepherd is responsible to feed his sheep. The pastor feeds the church membership by the preaching and teaching the Word of God. John 6:48 quotes Jesus Christ who says, "I am that bread of life." And 2 Timothy 4:2 tells the Pastor when to feed and how to feed by saying, "Preach the word; be instant in season, out of season; reprove, rebuke, exhort with all longsuffering and doctrine."

On some occasions a military commander is ordered to take Command of a unit he does not want to be associated with. And some military commanders will do anything or go anywhere at any expense or any cost to get promoted, even when it will compromise their personal integrity and character. But the pastor who has been called by God has different orders from 1 Peter 5:2, "Feed the flock of God which is among you, taking the oversight thereof, not by constraint, but willingly; not for filthy lucre, but of a ready mind."

A pastor is also to heed the church or flock which is the duty of a Bishop. He takes heed of the church, himself and the church members. Acts 20:28 tells the Pastor, "Take heed therefore unto yourselves, and to all the flock, over the which the Holy Ghost hath made you overseers…" And the next verse (29) warns, "For I know this, that after my departing shall grievous wolves enter in among you, not sparing the flock." The Pastor is responsible to be vigilant in watching for Satan's attacks on individual church members, the church, and false teachers.

Just as the military commander is responsible for his soldiers and unit, the pastor has the same duty and will give account to the Chief Shepherd, Jesus Christ.

Leadership on the Battlefield and in the Home

"No man that warreth entangleth himself with the affairs of this life; that he may please him who hath chosen him to be a soldier."

– 2 Timothy 2:4

The Army defines leadership as "the process of influencing others to accomplish the mission by providing purpose, direction, and motivation." Purpose gives soldiers a reason why they should do difficult things under dangerous, stressful circumstances; direction gives soldiers an orientation of tasks to be accomplished based on the priorities set by the leader; motivation gives soldiers the will to do everything they are capable of doing to accomplish a mission.

Army leadership is developed by training and experience at all levels of command, from a Major General who commands an Infantry Division to a Staff Sergeant who has direct command authority over a squad of soldiers, to a Sergeant who has direct command authority over a fire-team.

It is the Squad and Team leader and their men who make direct contact with the enemy. When these infantry squads and teams accomplish their individual mission, the platoons, the companies, the battalions, the brigades, and the divisions accomplish theirs. We will study the training of these leaders on the lethal battlefield and how their training relates to the spiritual battlefield.

It is somewhat easy to be a leader in private industry, whether it is factory work or outside labor, education, or civil service, but being a leader on today's lethal battlefield is not so easy. A poor decision by a combat leader will not cost the company, school, or community money but may result in lost lives. There is a certain stress level that goes along with private sector leadership but in combat the stress level is beyond calculation. In conventional warfare the combat leader's stress is elevated the closer he and his men are to the enemy lines (the forward edge of the battle area). In unconventional or guerilla warfare there are no lines, the enemy is all around you, he is not in uniform and is not identified until he fires at you. Spiritual warfare for the Christian family is just as lethal as unconventional warfare is for the soldier and his combat leader.

Small unit combat leadership training is critical for battlefield success. When every fire team, every squad, every platoon, and every company defeats the enemy on the field of battle, then every battalion and division will accomplish their mission. If one or two small unit leaders fail it is possible the entire battalion and division will fail. It is equally important for the Christian family to have the same level of combat leadership for their survival and success on the spiritual battlefield. Every family member is important just as every infantry squad member is important.

A combat leader must know battlefield tactics as it relates to the enemy and terrain. He must know how to maneuver his team in battle drills, offensive and defensive operations, security operations, and the planning, writing, and execution of operations orders. These are only a few of the tasks that the combat leader must master and execute while under enemy direct or indirect fire.

The Christian warrior must be just as proficient as the infantry combat leader. The leader is responsible for his family's safety in the home, to and from the workplace, and to and from school. He must be able to not only identify the enemy but he should also know his tactics; where the enemy is most likely to set ambushes, the type of ambush, how to maneuver his family out of the kill zone and danger areas, and how to counter attack. These critical skills are necessary for survival on the spiritual battlefield but the Christian warrior must also be able to provide purpose, direction, and motivation to each family member so they can be successful in accomplishing their mission.

One important task that every combat leader must master is the Land Navigation course. This task is so critical that all Army leadership schools begin with this subject and the "candidate" must demonstrate his proficiency. If a soldier fails the Land Navigation written exam or the day and night compass course he will be dropped from the leadership course. To lead his men to their objective the leader must be able to navigate, day or night, in any type of terrain using a map and compass. The leader must be able to choose the safest route to and from the objective, identify potential danger areas, identify terrain features that would hinder their march, select rally points, emergency extraction points, etc., all by conducting a map study. Then the leader must be able to lead his men to the objective by map and compass, accomplish the mission and return to their base of operations. The land navigation course is designed to test the potential leader in his navigational and leadership skills.

The "candidate" must pass a map reading examination that tests his knowledge of topographical map colors and what they represent, military symbols, the three types of contour lines and how their shape indicates terrain features, how to measure horizontal and vertical distance, the three norths, and how to use a lensatic compass. The hardest portion of the land navigation course is the day and night practical exercise. This is where the candidate is given a map and compass and he must successfully find numbered stakes in the ground as he travels a prescribed course or lane. There can be eight stakes in a lane and the lane can be 10,000 meters long, with several direction (or azimuth) changes.

An example would be: "From point 'A' travel 3,300 meters at an azimuth of 110 degrees. What lettered stake is located there?" This continues until the candidate locates all the stakes in his lane. The course is given more difficulty by having the student travel over different types of terrain. When this has been done the student must know his exact pace count per one hundred meters over flat and even terrain, uphill and downhill, and over rocky terrain. The student must count his steps accurately as there may be a lettered stake at the 2900 meter distance which would be incorrect. There is a day and night phase to the compass course. This map test and practical land navigation course is given in the first portion of a combat leader course. If the candidate does not know how to get from point "A" to point "B" by himself he will never be able to lead men to an objective under stressful combat conditions.

It is equally important for the Christian leader to know how to navigate on the spiritual battlefield. To avoid the snares of Satan, the husband or house hold leader must be able to navigate not only himself but also his family safely from home to work, to sport events, to social events, taking children to school and social events, on vacations, to church and everywhere in-between. Just as the driver of a vehicle must abide by all the rules of the road the Christian warrior must abide by the rules of spiritual warfare to get from point to point for we know that Satan is "going to and fro in the earth, and from walking up and down in it…looking for who he may devour" (Job 2:7, 1 Peter 5:8). Just as the combat leader must be able to identify safe routes, terrain features, rally points and danger areas for his team by a map study; the Christian warrior must be able to do the same for himself and his family. If the combat leader on the unconventional battlefield cannot find or get to his objective he will never accomplish his mission. It is the same for the Christian warrior if he takes the wrong route, if he gets hindered by social or political meetings on the spiritual battlefield.

Successful leadership on the spiritual battlefield is just as important as it is on the conventional battlefield. A unit's success is a result of the understanding of the principles of warfare, knowing the enemy and his intentions, and having trained and disciplined soldiers who trust and obey those placed in authority over them. The Spiritual battlefield, much like the unconventional battlefield is filled with danger. The unseen enemy is lurking everywhere, watching and waiting patiently for an opportunity to attack. And when soldiers are careful, watchful, and circumspect in everything they do, as they should, the enemy will set alluring and seductive booby traps to hinder and disrupt mission accomplishment.

Our soldiers today in Iraq and Afghanistan are fearless. They have confidence in their abilities as a result of their intense training, their weapons and equipment, and their leaders; and when needed they have the might, power, and combined resources of the entire U.S. military at their disposal.

The Christian warrior has even more at his disposal and can stand just as fearless. As an example, when Israel marched into the Promised Land the Amorites and Canaanites were already fearful of them. Joshua 2:9-10 describes the terror of the people and verse eleven says, "… our hearts did melt, neither did there remain any more courage in any man, because of you…" And Deuteronomy 11:25 says, "…for the Lord your God shall lay the fear of you and the dread of you upon all the land…", and 28:7 says, "The Lord shall cause thine enemies that rise up against thee to be smitten before thy face…and flee before thee…" By faithfulness, obedience to the Word, and promises of God, Israel entered the Promised Land fearlessly. Joshua 11:23 says, "So Joshua took the whole land according to all that the Lord said…"

The Biblical promises given to Israel apply to the Christian warrior on the spiritual battlefield today.

God provides purpose, provision, and protection to His leaders. The Christian warrior who heads the family and home must be just as determined as Joshua in the accomplishment of his mission. He must look out for the safety and welfare of the family unit, he must sound the alarm against attacks, he must ensure each family member is competent with their Sword (the Bible), that they are engaged in the work of the ministry and doers of the Word, and that they have the tools they need for mission accomplishment.

An infantry combat leader must also be decisive. On the field of battle decisions cannot always be by consensus as in the civilian world of private enterprise or civil service. Decisions may have to be immediate and executed immediately by soldiers who have faith and trust in their leaders.

There are many different approaches to the business method of decision making. Let us review a seven step method that is used:

- Step one: Outline your goal. This allows the decision makers to keep on track.

- Step two: Gather data. This helps the decision makers with a solution.

- Step three: Brainstorm to develop alternatives. Have more than one possible solution.

- Step four: List the pros and cons of each alternative. Eliminate alternatives with more cons than pros.

- Step five: Make the decision after analyzing each possible solution. Pick the one that has more pros than cons and one that everyone can agree with.

- Step six: Immediately take action once the decision is picked.

- Step seven: Supervise and reflect on the decision making process. This allows you to see what you did right and wrong.

The 7-step military decision making process is used for battalion size units and larger. These large organizations have staff officers in S1/personnel, S2/intelligence, S3/operations, and S4/logistics as a minimum. These staff officers make recommendations to the commander as to how the mission is to be executed. The process is somewhat similar to the business method that we have briefly reviewed. The seven steps are: Receipt of mission, mission analysis, development of courses of action, analysis of courses of action, courses of action comparison, course of action approval, and orders production. Development of the courses of action is in a broad general sense somewhat like the "pros and cons" used in the business model.

For the team or squad size unit the military uses a process called "troop leading procedures" which can be used for a family on the spiritual battlefield today. The eight steps are briefly outlined here:

- Step 1: Receive the mission. Identify what is going to be accomplished, what is known about the enemy, how terrain and weather will affect the operation, what troops are available, and how much time is available.

- Step 2: Issue a warning order. The order identifies all participants, the time the operation is to begin, and the time and place for the issuance of the actual operation order.

- Step 3: Make a tentative plan. This consists of a tentative course of action to take to accomplish the mission.

- Step 4: Start necessary movement. Subordinate leaders prepare men, weapons and issue necessary equipment for the mission.

- Step 5: Reconnoiter. The leader makes a personal reconnaissance to verify his map analysis, adjusts his tentative plan, and confirms routes and critical movements.

- Step 6: Complete the plan. The plan is completed based on the leader's personal reconnaissance.

- Step 7: Issue the complete order. The leader issues the operations order to all personnel and assigns individual tasks. He ensures the unit understands the concept and how the mission is to be executed.

- Step 8: Supervise. The leader supervises the squad's preparation for combat by conducting rehearsals and inspections.

The Christian combat leader who is leading his family into, across, and through the lethal spiritual battlefield must also be decisive in his decision making. The decisions he makes will affect each family member and the overall family mission. His decisions will affect the here and now for the entire family, and for all eternity. The born-again believer's decision making process is not based on the pros and cons of multiple courses of action, nor is it based on men, materials, time or money. The Christian warrior bases his decision making on the Word of God, his fear of the Lord, and the command to follow and obey.

There are numerous Biblical examples of decisions based on statements such as, "Thus saith the Lord..." and "The Word of the Lord came..." The commands that follow these statements do not always appear reasonable and most sound ridiculous, but when followed the outcome is always more than can ever be imagined. Isaiah 55:8-9 sums it up best when God says, "For my thoughts are not your thoughts, neither are your ways my ways, saith the Lord. For as the heavens are higher than the earth, so are my ways higher than your ways, and my thoughts than your thoughts."

The city of Jericho and its fall is an excellent example of spiritual leadership in combat. Jericho was a Canaanite stronghold and probably the most prominent city in the region. It was strategically located to control the ancient trade route from the east to Palestine. Its fall would open up the entire Promised Land to Israel. It was defended by an experienced army and mighty men of valor; it had high thick walls surrounding it. In Joshua 6:2 the Lord said unto Joshua, "…See, I have given into thine hand Jericho, and the king thereof, and the mighty men of valor." In the next few verses the Lord gives Joshua the tactics to use (verses 3-5), "And ye shall compass the city, all ye men of war, and go round about the city once. Thus shalt thou do six days. And seven priests shall bear before the ark seven trumpets of rams' horns: and the seventh day ye shall compass the city seven times, and the priests shall blow with the trumpets. And it shall come to pass that when they make a long blast with the rams' horn, and when ye hear the sound of the trumpet, all the people shall shout with a great shout; and the wall of the city shall fall down flat, and the people shall ascend up every man straight before him." Joshua did exactly as the Lord commanded and verses 20-21 say, "…and the people shouted with a great shout, that the wall fell down flat, so that the people went up into the city, every man straight before him, and they took the city. And they utterly destroyed all that was in the city…"

Another excellent example of how the Christian warrior is not to weigh pros and cons in his or her decision making, but to trust, follow, and obey the Word of God, is found in the book of Ruth. Ruth was from Moab, a country just east of Jordan, who married a son of Elimelech and Naomi of Bethlehem. Elimelech's two sons married Moabite women after he moved his family to Moab when there was a famine in Bethlehem. After ten years Elimelech and both of his sons died and his widow Naomi decided to move back to Bethlehem. This is where we observe the decision making process the two daughters-in-law go through in deciding to stay in Moab or return to Bethlehem with their mother-in-law Naomi. Let us weigh the pros and cons of their circumstances.

Pros to stay in Moab:

- First: Their entire family and friends lived in Moab.

- Second: When Naomi left they could return to their immediate loving family.

- Third: They could easily get a job if needed.

- Fourth: They would have an excellence chance to remarry.

- Fifth: They would be honoring Naomi's wishes for them to stay.

Cons to move to Bethlehem:

- First: All Moabites were hated by Jews. Deuteronomy 23:3-4 says, "An Ammonite or Moabite shall not enter into the congregation of the Lord; even to their tenth generation shall they not enter into the congregation of the Lord for ever: Because they met you not with bread and with water in the way, when ye came for out of Egypt; and because they hired against thee Balaam the son of Beor of Pethor of Mesopotamia, to curse thee."

- Second: Both daughters would have to travel with Naomi approximately eighty miles which would be a dangerous trip for three women.

- Third: Both daughters would have to find work so they could support themselves and Naomi.

Orpah decided to stay in Moab as would any person whose decision making process involves pros and cons. Naomi tells Ruth in chapter 1 verse 15, "And she said, Behold, thy sister-in-law is gone back unto her people, and unto her gods: return thou after thy sister-in-law." Ruth decided to leave with Naomi. In the next verse (16) she says to her mother-in-law, "...Entreat me not to leave thee, or to return from following after thee: for whither thou goest, I will go; and where thou lodgest, I will lodge: thy people shall be my people, and thy God my God: Where thou diest, will I die, and there will I be buried: the Lord do so to me, and more also, if aught but death part thee and me."

In the next few chapters of the book of Ruth we find that she works in Bethlehem supporting herself and Naomi, that she marries Boaz her kinsman-redeemer (Deuteronomy 25:5-10), her son Obed is the father of Jesse who is the father of King David. When you read the genealogy of Jesus Christ in the first chapter of Matthew verses 1-17, verse 5-6 say, "And Salmon begat Boaz of Rachab; and Boaz begat Obed of Ruth; and Obed begat Jesse; and Jesse begat David the king..." Then verse 16 says, "And Jacob begat Joseph the husband of Mary, of whom was born Jesus, who is called Christ." You find Ruth in the genealogy of King David and Jesus Christ. You find her name in this holy prestigious genealogy because she made her decision based not on pros and cons but on her love for her mother-in-law and her God. For ten years she witnessed the answered prayer, the faithfulness, the trust, the life and behavior of Naomi toward her God, and she wanted the same for herself.

As Joshua and Ruth, the Christian warrior must make his decisions based on the Word of God, not on the norms of society, not on current trends or traditions, and not on pros and cons relating to the circumstances of life. The Word of God is not like the smart books or procedure manuals of business, nor is it like the technical or training manuals of the military. The Word of God provides life-giving truth. Truth can never be changed. What was true in biblical times is still true today. Hebrews 4:12 says, "For the Word of God is quick, and powerful, and sharper than any two edged sword, piercing even to the dividing asunder of soul and spirit, and of the joints and marrow, and is a discerner of the thoughts and intents of the heart." 2 Timothy 3:16-17 says, "All scripture is given by inspiration of God, and is profitable for doctrine, for reproof, for correction, for instruction in righteousness: That the man of God may be perfect, throughly furnished unto all good works." Every circumstance of life is addressed in the Word of God. Ecclesiastes 1:9 says, "The thing that hath been, it is that which shall be; and that which is done is that which shall be done: and there is no new thing under the sun."

The Christian warrior in the leadership position on the spiritual battlefield must know his manual, the Bible, he must be in the Word each day, and he must fear the Lord, follow and obey His commands. Just as the military leader is praised by his subordinates because he "goes by the book" the Christian warrior must also "go by the Bible" in all that he does. The Christian must read and study the Bible to become a leader who "goes by the Book." 2 Timothy 2:15 says, "Study to shew thyself approved unto God, a workman that needeth not to be ashamed, rightly dividing the word of truth." Just as the military leader is promoted and praised for following and obeying orders the Christian warrior will also get his reward. Psalm 147:11 says, "The Lord taketh pleasure in them that fear him…," Jeremiah 42:6 says "…we will obey the voice of the Lord our God, to whom we send thee; that it may be well with us, when we obey the voice of the Lord our God." John 12:26 says, "If any man serve me, let him follow me; and where I am, there shall also my servant be: if any man serve me, him will my father honour," and Revelation 22:12 says, "And, behold, I come quickly; and my reward is with me, to give every man according as his work shall be."

A soldier who has demonstrated his technical and tactical proficiency meets one of the prerequisites for promotion. He must also display a desire and ability to train others, leadership skills, and he must be a graduate of the Primary Leadership Development Course. Infantry Corporals today usually make Sergeant on their second three year enlistment and they usually have had a one year deployment in Iraq or Afghanistan. To make Staff Sergeant (Squad Leader) the Sergeant must also be technically and tactically proficient in his specialty at his grade and must have been a successful Team Leader. Many enlisted soldiers today have college course work and some have college degrees prior to their enlistment. But they still begin their Army career as Privates and do not become Non-Commissioned Officers until they have demonstrated the proficiency, leadership skills, and gained the practical experience in the field.

Remember what we learned about the Forward Edge of the Battle Area or FEBA, and that the closer a soldier is to this line the more danger he is in. Combat Arms soldiers led by their Sergeants and Staff Sergeants are not behind this line, the positions they hold are the line. Survival and mission accomplishment for the infantry team and squad on today's lethal battlefield requires weapons proficiency and the leader's desire and ability to learn and train his team members.

The ultimate goal of the infantry squad and team leader is to destroy the enemy. To do this the infantry leader must look out for the welfare of his soldiers, ensure they have the proper equipment, that they are prepared physically and mentally for battle, and properly trained in tactics and weapons. On the battlefield the squad and team leader must take charge and lead their men around and through danger areas where they may be exposed to enemy observation and weapons; detect and avoid enemy ambushes, improvised explosive devices (IED's), booby traps and land mines; and defeat the enemy at the objective. All the while the infantry leader must display proper leadership skills that give confidence to his soldiers and provide purpose, direction, and motivation to his men until the mission is accomplished.

Leadership in the home is not too much different than leadership in the military, and is just as important, just as vital, just as critical, if not more so. A civilian leader, just as a military leader is not born a leader, leadership is learned and earned. Some men and women are born with a personality that draws others to them and they are popular, but this does not make them leaders. Some men and women have a natural talent in sports that draws others to them, but this does not make them leaders. Leadership is developed by education, knowledge, and experience.

The Army leadership school at Ft. Benning, GA. has its motto over the entry gate which says, "Follow me." Soldiers quickly learn the rest of the well know phrase Follow me "and do what I do." The Christian is given the same advice. Beginning with Matthew 4:19, Jesus said "And he saith unto them, follow me, and I will make you fishers of men," the phrase "follow me" is repeated by Jesus numerous times in the New Testament. In the book of James 1:23 Christians are told to be "..a doer of the word…," and in verse 25 we are told to be a "…doer of the work…"

One of the greatest followers in Scripture who went on to become one of the greatest General's in Scripture was Joshua the son of Nun. He was Moses' right hand man from the time Israel left Egypt and never left his side through the forty years in the wilderness. When God refused for Moses to cross the Jordan River he called Joshua to lead his people into the Promised Land. Directed by God, Joshua led Israel into battle and defeated the Amorites, the Perizzites, the Cannanites, the Hittites, the Girgashites, the Hivites and the Jebusites. Joshua was faithful to the Lord. He did all he was asked and that is what every servant leader should do.

With these examples we can now discuss leadership in the home. A husband and father is in the same position of a team or squad leader. A single mother may also be the leader of the home. The husband and wife team may have a family equal in size to a team (5) or squad (10) of soldiers. And it is their responsibility to provide purpose, direction, and motivation to the entire family. If you're the leader of your home what is your family mission? Do all family members know the mission? Do you provide the purpose, direction and motivation to the family to ensure mission accomplishment? Have you ever thought about it? Do you have a family or life verse? When speaking of a family mission it is more than just to insure they have security, clothing, and enough to eat. A family mission statement defines how the family will serve the Lord.

Joshua 24:15 may be used as a family mission statement, "And if it seem evil unto you to serve the Lord, choose you this day whom ye will serve, whether the gods which your fathers served that were on the other side of the flood, or the gods of the Amorites in whose land you dwell: but as for me and my house we will serve the Lord." If serving the Lord is your family's mission statement it should be posted on the walls at home as a constant reminder. Ecclesiastes 12:13 says, "Let us hear the conclusion of the whole matter: Fear God, and keep his commandments: for this is the whole duty of man." Serving and obeying the word of God is a duty, it is the whole duty, and it is a sacred duty. Verse 14 says, "For God shall bring every work into judgment, with every secret thing, whether it be good, or whether it be evil." This verse reminds us that all our work, good and bad, will be judged and we will give a personal account to God. This personal accounting is much like a military "After Action Report" at the conclusion of a mission. The best way for a family to serve the Lord is through His local New Testament church. Every New Testament local church has numerous ways to serve through different ministries. Such as: door knocking on Saturday mornings, visiting the church first time visitors, visiting church members who are ill, preaching and teaching in the local county jail, joining the choir, working in the nursery, discipleship training, greeting church guests on Sunday morning, serving as an usher, teaching Sunday school, building and grounds maintenance, kids Master's club leader, etc. There is a church ministry for every member of the family to serve.

Direction should be provided to all family members how to serve, where to serve and when to serve. As the leader of the household you should know the strengths and weaknesses of each family member and know their likes and dislikes, just as a military team leader and squad leader know their men. Just as the military leader gets direction and counsel from his chain-of-command the family leader should get additional direction and counsel from the Pastor of his local church. The book of James chapter one tells Christians to be "doers of the Word" and "doers of the Work." Who better to receive direction about when and where to serve in the church than the Pastor?

Military leaders are self-motivated but they must also motivate each of their soldiers every day until the mission is complete. Just as a Army leader must attend every military formation, the husband and leader has to motivate the entire family to not only attend all church services but also to serve.

What is your leadership style? In a broad general sense there are three leadership styles. First, the bully: it's always his way or the highway. He does not ask you to do something, it is always an order. He is quick to make a decision even if it's wrong. Second is the weak or timid leader: He is a sometimes leader. He often asks for suggestions and just about always seeks a consensus, not wanting to get anyone angry or upset. If possible he will let someone else take the leadership role, especially when things are going wrong. Third are those who are servant leaders who lead by example (as the military leader): Orders are more suggestive but he always expects them to be accomplished. Time permitting, he asks for suggestions and recommendations but always makes the final decision. He takes part in the process of work or mission to be accomplished and is always planning for the next mission.

A military commander has a command staff which consists of the commander, executive officer or chief of staff, personnel officer, intelligence officer, operations officer, and logistics officer. The commander uses his staff and always takes time to listen to their suggestions and recommendations. The commander relies heavily on his chief of staff who is in constant contact with every staff officer on a daily basis. While the commander is involved in future and current operations and the daily battle, his staff is coordinating time, equipment, and personnel for the next week, future operations or the next battle.

A husband, as the leader of the home, should never make a family decision without getting input from his wife or "chief of staff." While he is involved in his daily work schedule his wife (much like a chief of staff) knows the status of the children, the day to day and future operations of the family (baseball game, school activities, etc.), and the logistical needs of the home. The Christian wife wants her husband to be the leader of the home, but she wants to have her suggestions and recommendations given full consideration for decision making.

Proverbs 31:10-31 describes the virtuous woman that every Christian wife and mother should strive to become. She is industrious, pleases her husband and gains her husbands confidence. In all affairs of the family she acts with prudence and discretion. She contributes to the household, she is not lazy, and she cares for him and the home all the days of her life. A husband who does not seek counsel from his wife is like a military commander who does not listen to his command staff: he is sure to fail.

Combat leadership is important. Men live and die on the battlefield and in training because of decisions made by leadership. But, leadership in the home is more important because your own family members may become KIA, MIA or WIA because of decisions made by the leader on the spiritual battlefield. Leadership in the home means a lot more than who controls the checkbook. All major purchases or getting into debt by credit card should be discussed and decided by both husband and wife. Some men may be thinking "I let my wife decide; I just go to work and bring in the money." Some say to themselves, "The more I work, the more overtime I put in the better the household will be." But, how much money you're making, the number of hours you're working, how high up the corporate ladder you climb, or what your title or military rank is, is not important. The apostle Paul wrote fourteen of the New Testament books, he was an important disciple and missionary. Do you remember what his trade was, how he made his living? He was a tent maker and this is only mentioned a few times in Scripture. I'm sure Paul was one of the best tent makers in Biblical times. But how he made a living and how he supported himself is not important. My job and your job are not important either. How high up the corporate ladder we climb is not important, or our military rank. What is important is how we served, how we performed our duty. Romans 14:12 says, "So then every one of us shall give account of himself to God."

Where you work and how you work is important in supporting yourself and family. 2 Thessalonians 3:10 says, "For even when we were with you, this we commanded you, that if any would not work, neither should he eat." Your employment and salary is for the welfare of yourself, family, and tithes and offerings.

Every military leader receives an annual report which evaluates him in the performance of his duties and responsibilities. This report has a great influence in his future assignments and promotions. Every Christian leader will give account and be evaluated by our Spiritual

Commander as to what type of leader we were on the spiritual battlefield. What type of father and husband we were, how we spent our extra time and money, and how we served our Lord and Saviour. At the end of our accounting we all would like to be told we were faithful as stated to the servant in Matthew 25:21, "His lord said unto him, Well done, thou good and faithful servant: thou hast been faithful over a few things, I will make thee ruler over many things: enter thou unto the joy of thy lord."

Just as the military leader is responsible to his commander for all that his men accomplish or fail to accomplish, the husband as leader in the home is also responsible for all the family accomplishes or fails to accomplish in service to our Spiritual Commander. And just as the military leader reports and provides an After Action Report after every mission, husbands will give our Commander an After Action Report as we give account for all we do or fail to do. Husbands will give account for many areas such as:

- What is the family mission?

- Does your family attend church every time the doors are open?

- Does your family attend Sunday Bible study?

- What programs are your children watching on television?

- What videos, movies, and music does your family watch and listen to?

- Who are your children's friends?

- Who decides what to do with extra time and money?

- Do your children dress modestly?

- Does your wife dress modestly?

All these charges will be to the husband rather than the wife. The husband is ultimately responsible for all family decisions. The wife will be judged and give account of the household areas she is responsible for. Part of her duties are to provide her husband with all family details so he can make knowledgeable and wise decisions. Yes, she can work and contribute to the household just as the Proverbs 31 wife had done. But she will not give account for family leadership.

The Soldier's and Leader's Manual

"And he took the book of the covenant, and read in the audience of the people: and they said, All that the Lord hath said will we do, and be obedient."

– Exodus 24:7

The Army has a manual for everything; an instruction manual for every piece of equipment, every weapon, and for every duty and task a soldier and leader must accomplish to survive and be successful on the battlefield. In Basic Training the soldier receives the Soldier's Manual of Common Tasks which are referred to as "warrior skills." This contains each task a soldier needs to master in order to survive on the conventional and unconventional battlefield. The soldier is tested and must receive a "Go" on each task in order to graduate from Basic Training. Page one of the manual is the Soldier's Creed which every soldier must memorize (enclosure #3). To successfully graduate from Army Basic Training the soldier must display proficiency in the areas of: individual conduct, first aid, chemical-biological-radiological and nuclear warfare, combat techniques of survival on the battlefield, navigation, communication, hand grenades and land mines, individual weapons, casualty reporting, defense measures, battle drills, and the laws of land warfare.

After eight weeks of Basic Training the soldier enters Advanced Individual Training for his military occupational specialty referred to as MOS Training. For the infantry soldier this is another eight weeks of training and again he is issued a MOS manual for his specialty. This manual contains each duty and task a soldier needs to master in order to accomplish his wartime specialty so that his unit can accomplish their mission on the battlefield. The soldier is tested and must receive a "Go" on each task in order to graduate from his Individual Advanced Training.

The "specialty" Soldier's Manual also includes duties and tasks for each level of leadership in his military specialty. As the soldier matures and gains experience he is promoted to Corporal, Sergeant and on up the rank structure of his service. As he is promoted, the soldier's duties and responsibilities expand within his specialty and he becomes a team leader, squad leader, platoon leader, etc. The Army leader can transfer leadership authority to a subordinate who displays MOS technical and tactical skills and leadership qualities, but he can never transfer leadership responsibilities. Army leaders are responsible for everything their team, squad, platoon, or company does or fails to do.

The civilian business world also has their manual. It is sometimes called the SOP (standard operating procedure), or the procedure manual, smart book, technical manual, etc. This book serves the same purpose as the military manual for the civilian employee in his chosen vocation. In addition to containing work related procedures it usually also includes the business mission statement and employee standards of conduct.

All facets of the soldier's training, military experience and personal life must be taken into consideration. Leadership applies not only to mission accomplishment but also to the men and their families. The leader must focus on purpose, direction, and the motivation of his soldiers to be successful on the battlefield. A soldier on the battlefield who has personal problems at home with his wife, children, finances, medical, etc., cannot focus on his wartime mission.

The book of Nehemiah provides a biblical example of Army leadership. In chapter one God places the mission of rebuilding the walls of Jerusalem on Nehemiah's heart. In chapter two God, through King Artaxerxes, provides all the materials Nehemiah will need to rebuild the walls. When he arrives at Jerusalem, Nehemiah conducts a nighttime team leader's reconnaissance of the destroyed walls, formulates a plan, gathers volunteers and gives the mission statement. This is also the beginning of ridicule from Sanballat, Tobiah, and Geshem. (There is always ridicule and opposition toward those doing the Lord's work.) In chapter three he organizes his army of volunteer families, giving specific missions to build portions of the walls and gates. Nehemiah knew every member of his army of volunteers. In chapter four the enemies scoff and mock the Jews, and conspire to fight and hinder their work. All the while Nehemiah prays to God for his protection and direction. Nehemiah orders all those working on the walls to work and fight for their brethren, their sons, daughters, wives and homes. He organized the volunteers so that fifty percent worked on the walls and fifty percent were armed and guarded the work. Every man worked with one hand and held a weapon in the other (just as today's combat engineers.) In chapter five the volunteers complain not of the work on the walls, nor the amount of hours they worked, but of their debt, mortgage and bondage to the lenders. The volunteer army of workers could not focus on the mission, so Nehemiah warned and rebuked the lenders who then gave restitution to the families and the mission continued. In chapter six Nehemiah contends with the craftiness and treachery of Sanballat, Tobiah, and Geshem who brought up false accusations and stopped the work. (Satan makes every attempt to disrupt God's servants in the ministry God has called them. He attacks every level of the ministry, from servant worker to servant leadership.) In Verse 15 of chapter six we learn "… the wall was finished in the twenty and fifth day of the month Elul, in fifty and two days."

The mission was accomplished as Nehemiah prayed and led his volunteers by providing purpose, direction, and motivation. As the leader, he looked out not only for the welfare and safety of his army but also for their family's welfare and safety. He knew every individual soldier and his family, the social community, the politics, the economy and how it affected his soldiers. Today's Army leaders also lead as Nehemiah and are involved not only in the soldier but also his family and community. Christian men who are husbands, fathers, and soldiers must also lead their family team in the same manner in order to accomplish their mission. It is the husband's duty to give his family their mission statement, then to lead his family team by providing purpose, direction, and motivation as Nehemiah. The husband is also responsible for the welfare and safety of the family. He is to keep the family focused on the mission not on politics, current events, social traditions nor trends, until the mission has been accomplished.

Just as Satan attempted to disrupt Nehemiah in the building of the walls of Jerusalem he also makes every attempt to disrupt every Christian family and their ministry. When Satan could not stop the building of the wall by attacking Nehemiah personally by social and political intrigue, he attacked the soldiers building the wall. He attempted this by social and economic means by using the money lenders and their usury practices. He also did everything he could to place the soldier's families in harms way. However, Nehemiah, by the power of prayer was able to overcome every attempt made by Satan and accomplished his mission.

There are also several types of military soldiers and leaders who are required to go the extra mile. There are a few soldiers who are referred to Biblically as "mighty men of valour" as in Joshua 1:14, "…but ye shall pass before your brethren armed, all the mighty men of valour, and help them." This term is used numerous times in Old Testament Scripture as in Joshua 8:3(1) and 10:7(2), and 2 Kings 24:14(3), 1 Chronicles 5:24(4) etc.

Today these "mighty men of valour" soldiers have volunteered for Special Operations units and are all Airborne qualified paratroopers before attending the eight week Ranger course at Ft. Benning, GA, or the year and a half Special Forces qualification course at Ft. Bragg, NC. A quick overview of the three week Airborne course conducted at Ft. Benning, GA., (which is only a prerequisite to Special Operations training) consists of the following: The first week called "ground week" the soldier is introduced to the parachute, reserve chute, weapons containers, wearing of the parachute and equipment, and learns the parachute landing fall referred to as "PLF." The second week called "tower week" the soldier makes exits from simulated aircraft while wearing all the equipment for a combat jump. From a 34 foot tower the soldier exits the mock door of a military aircraft wearing a parachute harness which is attached by a fifteen foot static line to a one hundred foot long cable that runs from the tower to ground level. The soldier is graded on his exit from the mock door and his actions in the air as he slides down the cable. The third week, "jump week," the soldier makes five parachute jumps from an aircraft in flight.

During ground week the soldier learns in detail how to make a right-left-forward, and rear PLF; how to roll his body in the correct direction and manner while wearing his combat equipment consisting of a reserve parachute, weapon, special equipment he has been assigned, and usually an eighty pound ruck sack; what immediate actions to take in case of a parachute malfunction; actions in the air to avoid entanglement with another jumper; actions to take if landing on a hazardous landing zone which include power lines, water, trees, or high winds. There are two types of parachute malfunctions: a total malfunction and a partial. With a total malfunction the reserve parachute is immediately activated. A partial malfunction is when there is a hole in the canopy or when a suspension line is over the canopy giving the soldier two small canopies, making his rate of descent faster than other parachutists. The soldier immediately activates his reserve chute using the "down and away" method. This is when the soldier reaches into the reserve chute pack and grabs as much canopy as possible and throws it down and away from his body so it will properly inflate and not get entangled with the main canopy or its suspension lines.

When a paratrooper is descending he must look out for and stay away from other jumpers to avoid entanglements in the air. If a collision in the air is imminent the paratrooper must use the "spread-eagle method" to bounce off another canopy or suspension lines. When there is a total entanglement (this is more of a possibility during a night jump) the soldier higher up moves to the lower soldier so they have eye to eye contact. Then they hold on to each other by their harness straps until they come into contact with the ground. Upon contact they release their grip and make a parachute landing fall away from each other.

Another possible danger while descending is when a paratrooper goes directly below another parachutist. The lower parachute "steals" the air from the upper parachute causing it to collapse. When this occurs the upper parachutist will descend rapidly and he must move his legs and feet as though he is walking on the lower canopy. This movement will cause the lower canopy to move away from the upper soldiers who then will free fall until his parachute re-inflates. This is especially dangerous when it occurs at a low altitude.

The final danger is the landing. Every paratrooper is competent in the parachute landing fall (PLF) or he would not continue into the jump week of airborne training. The paratrooper is taught emergency landing procedures for the possible landing in or through a tree, water landing, hitting power lines, and high winds. There is a procedure to follow for each one of these potential hazardous landings that will save the soldier from serious injury or death.

During tower week the soldier simulates each emergency on the ground, in the air, and in the aircraft (as each type of aircraft has its own peculiar dangers) and what actions to take on each type of dangerous landing.

Emergency procedures that are not followed properly may result in serious injury or death to the jumper or a fellow jumper. Tower week consists of practice-practice-practice and rehearse-rehearse-rehearse until each action is so repetitive that it has been not only memorized by the soldier but also by his muscles. Memorized so that when the soldier is in a dangerous situation he does not have to think about the correct action to take but his mind and body will do the right thing automatically without thinking.

Jump week consists of making five successful static line jumps from an aircraft in flight. Four of the jumps are usually during the day without combat equipment. The fifth and last jump is a combat equipment jump. Usually two jumps are made on a Monday, another two jumps on Tuesday, and the last jump and graduation is on Wednesday morning. Thursday and Friday is only used if weather delays occur on Monday or Tuesday.

The Airborne school at Ft. Benning teaches mass tactical jumps similar to World War 2 where entire Airborne Divisions landed on "hot" (enemy shooting as the paratroopers are descending) drop zones. All Airborne training at Ft. Benning, GA, is still conducted in the same manner and using "static line" parachutes. The term "static line" means that a fifteen foot nylon line is attached to the apex of the parachute and is attached to the anchor line cable inside the aircraft. As the paratrooper exits the aircraft the line deploys out its length, the weight of the soldier deploys out the parachute from its back pack, then a small string breaks the parachute and jumper from the static line which is still attached to the inside of the aircraft, then the parachute fully deploys. The average paratrooper making an equipment combat jump weighs two hundred and fifty pounds with an average rate of descent of eighteen feet per second. All static line jumps from high performance aircraft are made from an altitude of twelve hundred feet. This minimum altitude is necessary as it allows the paratrooper to exit the aircraft, count four seconds before he visually checks to ensure his parachute is fully deployed. If the main chute has a total malfunction or is not fully deployed he still has time and altitude to activate his reserve parachute, for it to deploy, release his combat equipment, and to prepare for a parachute landing fall. At twelve hundred feet the average time in the air is sixty seconds.

Airborne training is physically and mentally intense. Soldiers must be alert, teachable, follow instructions, and able to overcome natural fears. They must learn, memorize, and demonstrate their mastery of each and every potential hazard that may occur from a parachute malfunction, deploying of the reserve parachute, actions in the air, and hazards on the drop zone that may cause serious injury or death to themselves or a fellow paratrooper. To exit an aircraft in flight from an altitude of only twelve hundred feet, to have a malfunction or to see a hazard, gives no time to think; the soldier must react immediately and instinctively to the hazard.

For every airborne operation the airborne commander appoints a "Jumpmaster" for each aircraft. The jumpmaster, regardless of rank, is delegated command authority and responsibility over all personnel and equipment in the aircraft. A jumpmaster is an experienced paratrooper, has displayed technical, tactical, and leadership skills, and must be a graduate of the Advanced Airborne course. The Jumpmaster's duties begin at the unit area where he briefs, inspects, and conducts pre-jump training. At the airfield he oversees parachute issue, inspects the aircraft, coordinates with the aircrew, and conducts the personnel inspection of every jumper on his aircraft. During the flight he enforces flight rules, issues time warnings, prepare door bundles, and issues jump commands. On the drop zone he accounts for all personnel and equipment and evacuates the injured.

To graduate from the Advanced Airborne course the student must pass a practical exercise as jumpmaster on his duties at the unit area, the airfield, in-flight duties, the main and reserve parachute, weapon and equipment containers, aircraft used in airborne operations, combat loads, and duties on the drop zone. He must pass a one hundred question final exam with a score of one hundred, and must perform a flawless jumpmaster inspection of five paratroopers in five minutes.

All military combat leaders utilize a Leader Handbook. This leader handbook is tailored to the leader's branch or military occupational specialty. It covers every contingency the leader will encounter within his specialty from administrative duties and responsibilities to combat related duties and responsibilities on the battlefield. If the leader is also a Jumpmaster he has an additional handbook that relates to his portion of the airborne operation. If, for example, there are twenty- five aircraft there will be twenty-five jumpmasters at the airfield. Because of the myriad of tasks that have to be conducted flawlessly at the airfield, in the aircraft and on personnel and equipment, the Jumpmaster always carries with him his Jumpmaster handbook which was issued to him on his first day of the Advanced Airborne course. This important and life saving handbook is often referred to as his Bible. Bible - because every word in the handbook must be followed to the letter, every task and procedure listed must be followed exactly as written, every aircraft utilized must be internally configured as depicted in the handbook, and every individual piece of equipment and weapon worn or carried by the paratrooper and every equipment door bundle must be prepared in the exact manner prescribed in the handbook. Failure to follow the Jumpmaster handbook will result in damaged aircraft, damaged or broken equipment on the drop zone, serious injury or death to the paratrooper, and ultimately the failure to accomplish the mission. Because the Jumpmaster handbook contains life and death instruction it is often referred to as the "Bible" by Christian and non-Christian jumpmasters.

Military leaders who are successful are frequently referred to by their subordinates, peers, and superiors as a leader who goes by the Book. He can always be depended upon in every situation to take a course of action, or to make a decision that is consistent with Army doctrine and training. When the military leader is not present to make on the spot decisions his subordinates know exactly what to do; "go by the Book." On the ever changing battlefield, when superiors are unable to make contact with a subordinate leader every soldier knows that in the absence of orders to go by the Book. Even when a new tactical situation presents itself the Leader's training will demand that he follow the military's format for the "Decision Making Process." He always goes by the Book.

The Book is Army doctrine, the Book is Army training, the Book teaches warrior skills, the Book teaches every Army specialty, the Book teaches leadership for the battlefield, the Book conducts safe airborne operations, the Book is every soldiers manual, the Book gets the soldier promoted, and the Book saves lives.

But, the Book is always changing. The principals of war never change but the weapons, weapons systems, and military technology change the tactical employment of the principals of war. So the Book changes as technology changes or a new Book is developed for the new weapon. Each and every military manual, handbook, or training circular contains a statement similar to this: "Users of this text are encouraged to submit recommended changes or comments which should be keyed to the page and line (s) of the text. Reasons should be provided to insure understanding and complete evaluation. Comments should be forwarded on Department Army Form 2028 and addressed to the Commandant." Army officers, non-commissioned officers, and trainers memorize great portions of the "Book" related to their military specialty to ensure military doctrine and training is followed, and to ensure the safety of personnel and equipment. Whenever a serious accident or death occurs in training an extensive investigation is conducted by a senior specialist in that particular field. The investigation determines fault in the equipment utilized, or on the individual using the equipment. These types of investigations all center on the Book: was it followed, not followed, or ignored?

The Christian leader, whether a pastor, deacon, teacher, father or husband also has a Book he can depend on. Where the military leader has a different leader book for his various duties and responsibilities the Christian has sixty- six books all wrapped up in one; the BIBLE. Where the military leader book may change due to weapons and their tactical deployment on the battlefield the BIBLE has never changed since it was written over two thousand years ago. It is current on every spiritual battlefield. Where the military leader book seeks recommended changes by its users the BIBLE tells every user in Deuteronomy 4:2, "Ye shall not add unto the word which I command you, neither shall ye diminish ought from it..." Where the military leader book teaches doctrine and training for every U.S. military specialty the BIBLE teaches doctrine and training for the entire scope of mankind's experience. Where the military leader book prevents serious injury or death, the BIBLE reveals that sin leads to death. Where the military leader book called the Uniform Code of Military Justice, can sentence men to federal prison or death, the BIBLE can free men from sin and give them everlasting life. Where the military leader book was written by knowledgeable experienced men and women in the military, the BIBLE was written by "...holy men of God who spake as they were moved by the Holy Ghost," 2 Peter 1:21.

Christian men and women should dedicate as much time to the Bible as military men and women dedicate to their leader book. The Christian leader should memorize important portions of the Bible as military leaders memorize important portions of their leader book. The Christian leader should dedicate time to teach Biblical doctrine to new converts as the military leader teaches military doctrine to new recruits. The Christian leader should dedicate time and energy to a disciple as the military leader mentors his replacement. Just as the paratrooper instinctively reacts to immediate danger due to his intense and repetitive training, the Christian should instinctively react to dangers on the spiritual battlefield. Just as the Jumpmaster trains, prepares, and equips all paratroopers on his aircraft, the Christian leader should train, prepare and equip his family team for the spiritual battlefield.

If investigations were conducted on Christian men and women who stop going to church, who have financial problems, who have employment problems, who have marital problems, whose children are rebellious, who divorce, who have social problems, who have addiction problems, etc., the findings would conclude that the BIBLE was not referred to nor its instruction followed. Further that the BIBLE was not read, the BIBLE was not memorized, the word of the BIBLE was not meditated upon, nor was the BIBLE considered sacred and life saving.

A military leader preparing himself and his men for combat on the conventional or unconventional battlefield would never forget his leader book because without it not only would he not survive on the battlefield but he would not be able to accomplish his mission. The Christian leader just like the soldier may have an important task or mission to accomplish. He may have all the time to accomplish it, he may have all the assistance he needs to accomplish it, and he may have all the resources needed to accomplish it, but if he cannot survive on the battlefield he will fail.

Army Leader Books are all written by men and pertain to specific military specialties. As stated earlier, as weapons, equipment, and tactics change and improve the leader books have to be re-written. The Bible was penned by men but authored by "holy men of God…as they were moved by the Holy Ghost" as stated in 2 Peter 1:21. The Old Testament was penned by prophets of God and the New Testament was penned by eye-witness apostles. The Bible never has to be rewritten because every single word is true and truth never changes. This is why the Bible's sixty-six books are in perfect harmony even though it was written over a period of sixteen hundred years by forty different writers. The Bible contains over three hundred prophecies of the birth of Jesus Christ, his life, his ministry, his resurrection and ascension and every one has been fulfilled. The Bible is the inerrant, infallible, preserved Word of God and contains truth to live by. 2 Timothy 3:16-17 says, "All scripture is given by inspiration of God, and is profitable for doctrine, for reproof, for correction, for instruction in righteousness; that the man of God may be perfect, throughly furnished unto all good works."

This Leader book for the Christian soldier addresses every personal, every social, every spiritual contingency in life that we face. The Bible says, "there is no new thing under the sun" (Ecclesiastes 1:9) and even when we think that no one has ever been in our situation ever before and there is no way out, even that is addressed in the Bible. 1 Corinthians 10:13 says, "There hath no temptation taken you but such as is common to man: but God is faithful, who will not suffer you to be tempted above that ye are able; but will with the temptation also make a way to escape, that ye may be able to bear it."

To give just one example of the all inclusive nature of the Bible let's look at some of the excuses and difficulties people give for not accepting the gift of salvation through Jesus Christ. Some may say, "I'm afraid I cannot live as a Christian." Philippians 1:6 says, "Being confident of this very thing, that he which hath begun a good work in you will perform it until the day of Jesus Christ." Or, "I have always been a Christian," John 3:3 says, "…Verily, verily, I say unto thee, Except a man be born again, he cannot see the kingdom of God." Or, "I'm not ready to give up worldly amusements." I John 2:15,17 says, "Love not the world, neither the things that are in the world, If any man love the world, the love of the Father is not in him….And the world passeth away, and the lust thereof: but he that doeth the will of God abideth for ever." Others may say, "I don't believe the Bible is the word of God." II Timothy 3:16 says, "All scripture is given by inspiration of God, and is profitable for doctrine, for reproof, for correction, for instruction in righteousness." Or, "I cannot forgive those who have hurt me." Ephesians 4:32 says, "And be ye kind one to another, tenderhearted, forgiving one another, even as God for Christ's sake hath forgiven you." Or, "I cannot give up my worldly friends." James 4:4 says, "Ye adulterers and adulteresses, know ye not that the friendship of the world is enmity with God? Whosoever therefore will be a friend of the world is the enemy of God." And some say, "I just cannot understand the Bible." I Corinthians 2:14 says, "But the natural man receiveth not the things of the Spirit of God: for they are foolishness unto him: neither can he know them, because they are spiritually discerned."

Or, "I believe there is nothing after death." Hebrews 9:27 says, "And as it is appointed unto men once to die, but after this the judgment." Or, "I believe everyone will go to heaven." John 3:36 says, "He that believeth on the Son hath everlasting life: and he that believeth not the Son shall not see life; but the wrath of God abideth on him." And many say, "God is too good to damn anyone." 2 Peter 2:4 says, "For if God spared not the angels that sinned, but cast them down to hell, and delivered them into chains of darkness, to be reserved unto judgment."

This is just one small example of the thousands of Scripture verses that provide God's everlasting truth to every circumstance of life. Truth never changes. What has been true in history, what is true today, what will be true in the future remains the same truth. There will never be a Bible Two or a Bible sequel because truth never changes.

The Leader book saves lives. The Bible not only saves lives on the spiritual battlefield but it gives everlasting life. Do you have any doubts of your personal salvation? Are you one hundred percent sure if you were to die today that you would go to heaven? Do you have a personal relationship with Jesus Christ? Let the truth of the Word of God set you free from this worry by following God's salvation plan:

- First: You must accept that you are a sinner.

  » Romans 3:23, "For all have sinned, and come short of the glory of God."

  » Romans 3:10, "As it is written. There is none righteous, no, not one."

- Second: You must accept that as a sinner you owe a penalty. That penalty is to be eternally separated from God the Father, and condemned to hell.

  » Romans 6:23, "For the wages of sin is death; but the gift of God is eternal life through Jesus Christ our Lord."

  » Ezekiel 18:4, "...the soul that sinneth, it shall die."

- Third: You must accept that Jesus Christ has already paid your sin debt by dying on the Cross and shedding his blood for you.

  » Romans 5:6, "For when we were yet without strength, in due time Christ died for the ungodly."

  » Romans 5:8-9, "But God commendeth his love toward us, in that, while we were yet sinners, Christ died for us. Much more then, being now justified by his blood, we shall be saved from wrath through him."

- Fourth: You must repent of your sins. Repent means to have a change of mind, to turn from sin and turn to Jesus Christ, or to make an "about face" from sin.

  » Acts 2:38, "...Repent and be baptized everyone of you in the name of Jesus Christ for the remission of sins, and ye shall receive the gift of the Holy Ghost."

  » Acts 8:22, "Repent therefore of this thy wickedness, and pray God, if perhaps the thought of thine heart may be forgiven thee."

- Fifth: You must accept that Jesus Christ has done it all for you and accept his gift of salvation.

  » Ephesians 2:8-9, "For by grace are ye saved through faith; and that not of yourselves: it is the gift of God: Not of works, lest any man should boast."

- Sixth: You must call on Jesus Christ to save you.

  » Romans 10:9,10, "That if thou shalt confess with thy mouth the Lord Jesus, and shalt believe in thine heart that God hath raised him from the dead, thou shalt be saved. For with the heart man believeth unto righteousness; and with the mouth confession is made unto salvation."

  » Romans 10:13, "For whosoever shall call upon the name of the Lord shall be saved."

If you have never called on Jesus Christ for his salvation I urge you to do it now. Get on your knees wherever you are and pray this type of prayer; "Dear Lord Jesus, I know I am a sinner, and I deserve to pay my own sin debt, but I do believe that you died for me to pay the debt that I owe. Today, the best I know how, I trust you as my Saviour. I will depend on You from this moment on for my salvation. Now help me to live for you and to be the Christian you want me to be."

Hard Target

"Wherefore take unto you the whole armor of God, that ye may be able to withstand in the evil day, and having done all, to stand. Stand therefore, having your loins girt about with truth, and having on the breastplate of righteousness; And your feet shod with the preparation of the gospel of peace; Above all, taking the shield of faith, wherewith ye shall be able to quench all the fiery darts of the wicked. And take the helmet of salvation, and the sword of the Spirit, which is the word of God."

– Ephesians 6:13-17

On the field of battle the enemy is always looking for an easy target. This is especially true in unconventional warfare because the enemy is not strong. He has few soldiers, limited firepower, limited mobility and resources to get around on the battlefield, and usually no reinforcements. So he saves his limited firepower for easy or soft targets and he never becomes decisively engaged. Decisively engaged is an engagement in which a unit is considered fully committed and cannot maneuver or extricate itself without outside assistance. A soft target is a person that is relatively unprotected or vulnerable, who has limited training or an untrained civilian, who is unable to defend himself properly, and no reinforcements available. Conversely a hard target is someone who moves about on the battlefield in such a way as not to present himself as an easy target to the enemy, who is well prepared and trained to engage the enemy, wears his body armor correctly, who is experienced and qualified in the use of the weapons of war and is well able to defend himself properly, with reinforcements close by.

For the Christian warrior the same targeting applies. Are you a hard or soft target? The soft target on the spiritual battlefield is a person who has no discipleship training, goes about without battle armor, who is not cautious in his movements, not cautious in his thoughts letting his mind wander, does not coordinate with team members or has none, and carries no weapons. The Bible teaches how to become a hard target in ten easy lessons:

- ■ *First,* put on the full armor of God. All soldiers deployed in Iraq and Afghanistan are living in military compounds or camps. These camps are isolated from the population by fortified eight foot thick walls, topped with razor wire, and each entrance is guarded 24/7 by trained security officers and soldiers. Soldiers eat, sleep, train, plan, and recreate in these fortified camps. Whenever any sized unit of soldiers leaves the camp (goes outside the wire) to support or conduct combat operations, they must wear battle armor. This consists of combat boots, helmet, armored vests with plates, individual weapons and ammunition, hand grenades, smoke grenades, medics, radios, rations, and water. Then they coordinate with the Tactical Operations Center regarding their mission and provide the date and time of return. Only then are the soldiers prepared for the battlefield. Prior to leaving the compound, each soldier is inspected by his team or squad leader to ensure he has everything needed to survive on the battlefield and is carrying the equipment necessary to accomplish the mission.

For the Christian to survive on the spiritual battlefield and accomplish his mission takes the same planning, coordinating, equipping, and weapon as the soldier. The Apostle Paul in Ephesians 6:11 takes each piece of armor a Roman soldier wears and makes a spiritual application for us. The verse says, "Put on the whole armor of God, that ye may be able to stand against the wiles of the devil." The word "wiles" in verse 11 is defined as "cunning arts, deceit, craft, or trickery." In 1 Timothy 3:7 Paul warns to be careful when he says, "…lest he fall unto reproach and the snare of the devil," and in 2 Corinthians 2:11 he warns, "Lest Satan should get an advantage of us: for we are not ignorant of his devices." Satan is crafty and uses trickery to snare his enemy on the spiritual battlefield just as terrorists today use IED's, mines, and booby traps to injure, maim and kill soldiers on the modern unconventional battlefield.

In Ephesians 6:13-17 Paul identifies each piece of armor and makes the application, "Wherefore take unto you the whole armour of God, that ye may be able to withstand in the evil day, and having done all, to stand. Stand therefore, having your loins girt about with truth, and having on the breastplate of righteousness; And your feet shod with the preparation of the gospel of peace; Above all taking the shield of faith, wherewith ye shall be able to quench all the fiery darts of the wicked. And take the helmet of salvation, and the sword of the Spirit, which is the word of God."

The first piece of armor mention in verse 14 says, "…having your loins girt about with truth…" The word "girt" refers to a girdle. A Roman soldier wore a belt around his waist which was used to hold other pieces of his armor in place, and the word "truth" refers to having the knowledge of the truth of God's Word. The second piece is the "breastplate of righteousness" also mentioned in verse 14. The breastplate protects the physical heart and lungs of the soldier. Spiritually, it refers to the Christian soldier who is robbed of this important piece of armor because of his unrighteous acts which will expose his heart to

Satan. The third piece of armor refers to the Roman soldiers' sandals in verse 15. He wore sandals which protected his instep and ankle and the soles were studded with nails for firm footing. This gave the soldier a willingness to advance toward the enemy. Similarly, this refers to the assurance and confidence a Christian soldier has in knowing the truth of the "gospel of peace." The fourth piece of armor is the "shield of faith" in verse 16. The Roman soldier carried a heavy oblong shield for his protection. This shield refers to the faith a Christian soldier has in the Word of God and His promises, and protects him from doubts induced by the trickery, deceits, and snares of Satan which are referred to as the "fiery darts of the wicked" in this verse. Since the darts of the wicked are in flames, if we are sober and vigilant (1 Peter 5:8) we will see them coming near and can avoid them. The fifth piece of armor is the "helmet of salvation" in verse 17. This protects the Roman soldier's head and brain. Spiritually this refers to the Christian soldier's cognitive certain assurance of salvation. The sixth and last piece of armor is "sword of the spirit." The sword is the Romans soldier's offensive weapon. Spiritually this refers to the Word of God which is also the Christian soldier's offensive weapon. The Word of God is how Jesus Christ defeated Satan when He was tempted by him for forty days in the wilderness in Luke chapter four and is also described in each of the Gospels.

As the infantry soldier awakes each morning, putting on all his combat equipment and weapon, he prepares himself for the daily battle. It is just as vitally important for the Christian soldier to put on the entire armour of God to prepare himself for the spiritual battlefield. Just as the squad or team leader inspects each soldier prior to going outside the wire the spiritual leader of the home should do likewise. The leader of the home is just as responsible for his family members as the infantry leader is of every member of his squad. If a squad member is not prepared nor equipped for the daily battle the squad leader will not allow him to leave the camp.

Is each member of your family properly trained and properly equipped for the daily battle at school or at work? Is each family team member a hard or soft target? It is the leader who is responsible for the training, mentoring, and inspection of every member of the family team.

- **Second**, keep your mind clear. The soldier on the lethal battlefield today must keep his mind free of personal distractions, social distractions, political distractions, and financial distractions so he can focus on his survival on the lethal unconventional battlefield and mission accomplishment. Keeping his mind free of distractions allows the soldier to memorize, meditate on, and execute the "operations order" that his unit is conducting on the battlefield. A small unit operations order is composed of five paragraphs. They are: situation (the friendly and enemy situation), mission, execution, service support, and last command and signal.

Every soldier on the mission must memorize portions of the "order" that pertain specifically to his MOS specialty and portions pertaining to assigned tasks within the squad. For example, if the soldier's specialty is communications and has been assigned as the squad radio operator he must memorize all radio call signs, the primary, alternate, and emergency frequencies, and ensure he is carrying enough additional batteries needed for the duration of the mission. This same radio operator must also memorize his additional duties and responsibilities that have been assigned him by his squad leader. For instance he may have additional duties of security of the left side of the squad during movements, he may be assigned as part of the assault team at the objective, and he also may be tasked to search enemy prisoners. In addition to this, just as every other squad member, he must memorize the challenge and password, and he may also be tasked to carry colored signaling flares, one hundred rounds of machine gun ammunition, a claymore mine, a block of plastic explosive, etc. As you can see, every soldier is an important member of the squad and during a mission he must have a clear mind and be focused on every duty and responsibility he has been assigned to ensure survival and mission accomplishment.

The squad and team leaders must memorize the entire operations order. Leaders know the mission and specialty of each soldier, their assigned duties and responsibilities and what special equipment each member is carrying. The leader must also know where each soldier is located within the squad during movement and at halts. The operations order also provides contingency plans for emergencies. A soldier who does not follow exact directions contained in the operation order may cause serious injury or death to himself or a team member or jeopardize mission accomplishment. A soldier must keep his mind clear whenever he is on the conventional or unconventional battlefield. His life and the life of his fellow soldiers depend on his knowledge of his specialty, his experience, and his focus on his duties and responsibilities in accomplishing his mission and the overall mission of his team.

Keeping a clear mind is just as important to the Christian warrior. Whenever he leaves his home he is entering the spiritual battlefield where Satan is walking about. His family is just as concerned for his safety and welfare as the Tactical Operations Center is concerned for a unit conducting combat operations on the unconventional battlefield. The Christian soldier can stay focused on his survival and mission by meditating on the Word of God just as the soldier meditates on his military manuals. I Peter 1:13 says "Wherefore gird up the loins of your mind, be sober..." and 1 Peter 5:8 says, "...be sober, be vigilant..." These verses teach the Christian to remain focused, to develop personal discipline and moral conduct. To be sober minded means to be serious, cool and calm in all things. Circumspect means to look around in every direction, to be cautious and careful of pending dangers. These military terms of sober minded, vigilance, and circumspect are "guard duty" terms for the protection of the soldier and his team members.

To keep his mind clear the Christian warrior must meditate on the Word of God daily. Psalm 1:2 says, "But his delight is in the law of the Lord; and in his law doth he meditate day and night." If you meditate on the Word of God and do what it says to do you will be blessed by God. Joshua 1:8 says, "This book of the law shall not depart out of thy mouth; that thou shalt meditate therein day and night, that thou mayest observe to do according to all that is written therein: for then thou shalt make thy way prosperous, and then thou shalt have good success."

A soldier who is not focused, whose mind is not clear about his duties and responsibilities on the battlefield is a danger to himself and his team members. And Paul warns Timothy in 2 Timothy 2:4, "No man that warreth entangleth himself with the affairs of this life; that he may please him who hath chosen him to be a soldier." An entanglement is anything that may confuse or cause disorder in the mind of the soldier. It may involve politics, government, sports, new events at home, gossip, or any other thing that will cause the soldier to be distracted or perplexed with the cares of the world. He must be clear minded to fight the daily battle and to please his commander.

- **Third**, be on-guard 24/7. Remember I Peter 5:8, "Be sober, be vigilant; because your adversary… walketh about, seeking whom he may devour." The meaning is for the soldier to be watchful, circumspect, and attentive to discover and avoid danger, and to provide for the safety of others. A soldier on the battlefield never lets his guard down because the results can be catastrophic. On today's unconventional battlefields like Iraq and Afghanistan the enemy never wears a uniform and hides his weapons. One of their tactics is to get as close as possible to U.S. soldiers and throw a hand grenade, bomb, or wear a harness full of explosives killing themselves and our servicemen. Another tactic is to drive a vehicle filled with explosives into a group of U.S. soldiers or into a building where soldiers have congregated.

Another enemy tactic is the planting of roadside bombs or IED's (improvised explosive device that can be remotely detonated) on the roads or roadways used by U.S. personnel. The enemy may also place explosives on vehicles that can be remotely detonated when a U.S. vehicle filled with soldiers comes near. Soldiers must remain alert for suspected enemy soldiers and the placement of IED's. There are technological countermeasures that may expose IED's but the individual experience and trained soldier must look for visual signs also. These signs may be recently turned-over soil or sand by a road, or an abandoned vehicle on the roadway, or a local native using a cell phone on or near the roadway. The enemy is innovative, he is determined, he is persistent, and he is patient because he is limited in personnel and weapons. He attacks only when he has the tactical advantage of surprise and an avenue of escape.

The soldier must be just as cautious, just as sober minded, just as vigilant, and just as circumspect when inside his own military compound. The enemy makes every attempt to infiltrate the "wire." If he cannot gain entrance by stealth, or by trick such as the wearing of an Afghanistan Army uniform or by posing as an Afghanistan civilian working on the U.S. compound, etc., he will fire mortars or rockets into the compound area. There are no one hundred percent safe areas on the battlefield.

The Christian on the spiritual battlefield must be just as diligent and just as sober as the soldier on the unconventional battlefield. When he leaves his home he must put on his armor and have his weapon, just as the soldiers in Iraq and Afghanistan are cautious when leaving the wire and are watchful for the enemy who blends in with the civilian population. The enemy uses the same tactics on the spiritual battlefield. The results may not be physically damaging but they will be spiritually damaging. Matthew 7:15 warns, "Beware of false prophets, which come to you in sheep's clothing, but inwardly they are ravening wolves."

Soldiers are also warned prior to deployment not to take war trophies or souvenirs. They will appear seductive and harmless but most are booby trapped with IED's and will kill or maim the soldier. The Christian warrior must also be cautious and avoid "things" that will be seductive and harmful to him. The seventh Proverb describes a young man who has no moral discipline and is seduced by a harlot "as an ox goeth to the slaughter or as a fool to the correction of the stocks." 1 John 2:16 warns, "For all that is in the world, lust of the flesh, and the lust of the eyes, and the pride of life, is not of the Father, but is of the world."

Even in the home the Christian soldier must be on guard. The enemy will make every attempt to gain entrance into the home and if he cannot enter he will send rockets into the home. The Christian must be on guard 24/7 against internet predators, on-line gambling, or seductive "X" rated television programs, movies, etc.

- **Fourth**, coordinate and fellowship with fellow Christian warriors. Acts 2:42 says, "And they continued steadfastly in the apostles' doctrine and fellowship, and in breaking of bread, and in prayers." Find and keep Christian friends to socialize with, study the Bible with, and pray one for another. Immediately upon enlistment a soldier is taught team work and the buddy system. In fact, many military service members join under the "buddy system." This is an enlistment that guarantees that two enlistees will attend Basic Training together. The buddy system is an integral part of Army training and is emphasized during all phases of training and continues throughout military service. Civilians join the military and come from all over America and all walks of life. The military service joins them together. They take an oath together, they train together, they live together, they serve together in peace time and at time of war, and they have a common bond that only the military service provides.

Within each military service there are many specialties. These specialties separate soldiers within the service they joined. In the Army for instance a soldier may become an infantryman, but there are many types of infantry. There are Infantryman, Indirect Fire Infantryman, Mechanized Infantryman, Air Assault Infantryman, Airborne Infantryman, and Airborne/Ranger Infantryman. Each of these has their own specialized training and Professional Development schools and Associations. Each type of infantryman stays in their chosen career specialty throughout their term of service. Every infantry branch has their own Army base so they continue their advanced training together but separated from the other types of infantry. For example, Infantry are usually based at Ft. Benning, GA, Mechanized Infantry are based at Ft. Hood, TX, Air Assault Infantry are based at Ft. Campbell, KT, Airborne Infantry are based at Ft. Bragg, NC. After Basic Training these different types of Infantry train together, live together, serve together, are deployed to combat zones together, and when necessary give their lives together.

It is the same for the Christian soldier on the spiritual battlefield today. After giving your life to Jesus Christ you have joined God's Army. You have been adopted into the family of God, and have been grafted into his family. Ephesians 1:5 says, "Having predestinated us unto the adoption of children by Jesus Christ to himself, according to the good pleasure of his will." Luke 2:13 uses the word "host" which refers to an army when he says, "And suddenly there was with the angel a multitude of the heavenly host praising God and saying..." Being part of God's army you were not drafted in but were "graffed" in, Romans 11:23 says, "And they also, if they abide not still in unbelief, shall be graffed in: for God is able to graff them in again."

Just as military service members get sworn in and take an oath, Christians should join, train, live, pray, and serve our heavenly Father together. Just as a military member, it does not matter where you are from, what color your skin is, or what walk of life you're from. If you're in God's army you're in the right specialty so, as the military does, let us give our lives to

Him. And just as military members look out for one another Christian soldiers must pray for each other. James 5:16 says, "Confess your faults one to another, and pray one for another, that ye may be healed. The effectual fervent prayer of a righteous man availeth much."

Just as the Airborne Infantry are stationed at Ft. Bragg, NC the born-again believer should station himself in a local New Testament church in the immediate area of his home. Most Christian churches have a written "Statement of Faith" that members sign to become church members. He should find a church where he can have fellowship, where he can pray one with another, and a location where he can share burdens. He needs a church where he can grow as a Christian, where he can help others grow, where he can train and train others, where he and his family are safe, secure, and can be comforted by the teaching and preaching of the Word of God by a pastor.

- **Fifth,** keep separate from non-Christians. The average American does not often see a military service member. Those who live near a military reservation often will see service members going to and from work, but they probably seldom socialize with them, as the majority of service members socialize primarily one with another.

The reason for this is that the average U.S. citizen does not fully understand the dedication, loyalty, faithfulness, commitment, pride and the willingness to work long hours without additional compensation that is often necessary for the military member. Many private citizens (not most) regard their employers and supervisors as selfish men and women who only use employees as tools to obtain the next bonus, or the next promotion up the corporate ladder. They look at the "corporation" as a profit making conglomerate that has no regard for the employees, and that their co-workers cannot be trusted because many of them only want to climb the corporate ladder and are not mindful of who they have to step on to get there.

Many employees today are always looking for a better employment package. If they are offered even one dollar more per hour or some added benefit they will leave their present employer. Few employees today expect to spend twenty or more years with the company they are working for. A minority of Americans think the serviceman is an uneducated country bumpkin who is not smart enough to get employment anywhere in the private sector or civil service; and view all service members as low class citizens and are grateful they do not have to serve in the military themselves. These same citizens have little in common with the service member.

The average service member has a much different reason for not socializing with John Q. American citizen. The soldier did not take the first job that came his way after high school or college, he chose and volunteered for the military. The American service member is a member of a team. Yes he is an individual and has personal duties and responsibilities but he is an important part of a team, and that team depends on him. His team leader cares about him and looks out for his welfare and the welfare of his family. His leader even helps him get his civilian and military education so he can meet the requirements for promotion.

The infantry soldier does not get the opportunity to attend work related conventions and seminars in large city convention centers where supervisors and co-workers are entertained after hours. The infantry soldier's continuing education is conducted in the training fields of Ft. Benning, and Ft. Bragg, where their training is conducted 24/7 for weeks or months at a time under simulated combat conditions. Where a co-workers error or slight mistake in the office or factory may be humorous, an error on the infantry training ground can result in a fatal training accident. The infantry soldier shares a common bond only with other soldiers. They have a common interest they have dedicated their lives to and are willing to give their lives for. America is free because of the brave service members who are willing to die for their country.

After that day of infamy, September 11, 2001, America embraced their military for what they have done immediately following and are continuing to do in Afghanistan and Iraq today. Service members are frequently approached and humbly thanked by the American public. This is an example of the infrequent exceptions to "separation" but overall it is mutually accepted and encouraged.

It is the same for the Christian warrior who is serving on the spiritual battlefield. Non-Christians think the born-again believer is an uneducated country bumpkin. Anyone who spends his free time on a Saturday morning visiting his neighbors inviting them to church, giving the Gospel, and spending all day Sunday in church; and giving his extra money in tithes and contributing to missions is a "whacked out Jesus freak." The believer and non-believer have nothing in common nothing to bind them together. They think exactly opposite of each other as light is to dark. 2 Corinthians 6:14 says, "Be ye not unequally yoked together with unbelievers: for what fellowship hath righteousness with unrighteousness? And what communion hath light with darkness?" 2 Corinthians 6:17 says, "Wherefore come out from among them, and be ye separate, saith the Lord, and touch not the unclean thing; and I will receive you." I Peter 1:15 says, "But as he which hath called you is holy, so be ye holy in all manner of conversation." The word "holy" in Scripture means to be set apart for sacred use. In this verse the word "conversation" refers to a person's pattern of behavior or lifestyle. The unbeliever changes truth to a lie. Romans 1:25 says, "Who changed the truth of God into a lie, and worshipped and served the creature more than the Creator, who is blessed forever." As the military warrior is separate from the civilian the Christian warrior is to keep separate from the non-believer.

The born again believer has been ordered to be separate but he has to live in the world. The principle of being holy in 1 Peter 1:15 that we just read means to be completely at God's disposal, ready for His use anytime, anywhere, and under any circumstance just as the combat soldier is today. Today's culture tempts man to live an immoral lifestyle. Single men and women living together as a married couple, casual sex, immodest and revealing dress, and the frequent use of foul language as examples are only a few reasons for separation.

2 Corinthians 5:20 refers to the Christian as an ambassador when it says, "Now then we are ambassadors for Christ, as though God did beseech you by us; we pray you in Christ's stead, be ye reconciled to God." An American ambassador is a representative of the United States to the country he is assigned to live. Even though he lives in a foreign country he is not a citizen of that country. His mission, simply stated, is to explain to the citizens of the foreign country all that is good in the United States and to promote it. This is the same mission of every born-again Christian as an Ambassador of Christ.

To reinforce separation Scripture frequently uses the terms stranger as in Matthew 25:35(1) and sojourner in Psalm 39:12(2). John 8:23(3) tells the Christian that he is "…not of this world…" and Romans 12:2 tells the born-again believer, "And be not conformed to this world but be ye transformed by the renewing of your mind…" and 1 Peter 2:11 calls Christians strangers and "pilgrims." The Christian soldier on the spiritual battlefield has been commanded to separate himself from the world but he is to live in the world as an ambassador of Christ.

- *Sixth*, always keep your weapon close at hand. Ephesians 6:17 reminds us, "…and the sword of the Spirit, which is the word of God." As you recall of all the armor of God the sword is the only offensive weapon, and it is referring to Scripture, the Bible. It was the only weapon used by Jesus Christ to defeat Satan while tempted forty days in the wilderness as described in Luke chapter four. At each temptation Jesus responded with Scripture as he did in Luke chapter four verse four, verse eight, verse twelve, and verse thirteen says, "And when the devil had ended all the temptation, he departed from him for a season."

Hebrews 4:12 says, "For the word of God is quick, and powerful, and sharper than any two edged sword…"

For the infantryman, beginning in Basic Training, his weapon becomes a part of him. Beginning with the American Revolution to the war in Iraq and Afghanistan today the warrior is never separated from his weapon. It is the first thing he sees and feels in the morning and the last thing he sees and feels when he goes to sleep . He knows every part of it, he assembles and disassembles it (he can do it blindfolded), he can name every part, he knows its capabilities and limitations, he understands how it functions, he knows how much it weighs and how long it is, he goes to the rifle range and qualifies with it at every opportunity, and he knows that his life and others are dependent on the care, maintenance, knowledge, and ability he has in using his weapon.

The M-9 is a 9mm semi-automatic pistol and is the standard handgun carried by the military in combat operations. It is also carried by Military Police officers on the battlefield and at their home base where they are permanently stationed. This M-9 (and similar type semi-automatics) is also carried by civilian law enforcement officers. These military and civilian law enforcement officers undergo extensive training in the laws of arrest, the use of force, and the use of deadly force while in the performance of their duties. The civilian term "deadly force" is similar to the military's "rules of engagement." All police officers must pass a monthly live fire pistol qualification course demonstrating their proficiency.

Every military or civilian law enforcement officer must be trained and ready to use his weapon for his self-protection and for the protection of others. When a military or civilian police officer responds to a robbery-in-progress call or if he is attacked while eating lunch he must respond to the threat appropriately. Having and carrying a weapon is a responsibility that should never be taken lightly. A weapon can take a life and it can save a life.

SURVIVAL ON THE SPIRITUAL BATTLEFIELD

It is the same for the Christian warrior on the spiritual battlefield with his weapon, the Word of God. Once he accepts Jesus Christ as his Lord and Savior, he picks up his two edged sword, the Bible. He should never get separated from it and always have it close at hand from the time he gets up in the morning to the time he goes to bed. He should know every part of the Bible. He can name all thirty-nine books of the Old Testament and that they are organized by the law books, history books, poetical books, and the prophetical books. He can name all twenty-seven books of the New Testament and that they are organized by the Gospels, history, epistles and prophetical.

Just as the combat veteran on the unconventional battlefield depends on his weapon to save his life and those of his unit, the Christian on the spiritual battlefield can depend on his weapon for the same purpose. The infantry soldier on the battlefield has a weapon that is well used, worn and scratched up. It is also well oiled and always ready for use. The Christian warrior's Bible should also be well used, worn and always ready for use. When everything goes wrong on the battlefield, when the operation order goes wrong and all contingency plans go wrong, when the enemy has surprised you, when there is no safe place to go, the soldier will always grab his weapon and make every attempt to accomplish the mission. He will never accept defeat, he will never leave a fallen comrade, he will never throw down his weapon and quit. The Christian warrior on the spiritual battlefield faces identical situations. When all your plans for employment, education, family and finances go wrong, it may seem as Satan has surprised you and there is no place to go; but as the infantry soldier you must place your mission and Jesus Christ first, never accepting defeat, never leaving a fallen Christian brother or sister. Never throw down your weapon the Bible, and never quit.

Just as the infantryman's weapon saves lives, the Bible, the Sword, the Gospel, the Word of God, and Scripture also saves lives. Terms the Bible uses in life saving situations are "quicken" which means to make alive, as in Psalm 119:154, "Plead my cause, and deliver me: quicken me according to thy word;" "Save" as in Mark 8:35, "...whosoever shall lose his life for my sake and the gospel's, the same shall save it;" "salvation" as in Acts 28:28, "...the gospel of Christ: for it is the power of God unto salvation to every one that believeth...;" "light" as in 2 Timothy 1:10, "...our Saviour Jesus Christ, who hath abolished death, and hath brought life and immortality to light through the gospel;" "everlasting" as in John 6:47, "...He that believeth on me hath everlasting life."

The Sword of God also directs the Christian warrior safely through the spiritual battlefield. Psalm 119:105 says, "Thy word is a lamp unto my feet, and a light unto my path." Psalm 32:8 says, "I will instruct thee and teach thee in the way which thou shalt go: I will guide thee with mine eye;" and Psalm 5:8 says, "Lead me, O Lord, in thy righteousness because of mine enemies...;"

The Word of God is the only offensive weapon of the believer. The Christian warrior should be just as knowledgeable, just as experienced, just as qualified, and just as ready to use this weapon on the spiritual battlefield as the infantry soldier on today's lethal battlefield.

One day at the Los Angeles County Recorder's office a large male in his early thirties entered. He had the physique of a football lineman and wore loose fitting short pants and a tank top. He had gang type tattoos on every exposed area of his body and on his face he had tears tattooed under his eyes. He looked all around the research area noting all the computers, then at shelf after shelf of the reels of microfiche, and with an irritated, frustrated look sat down next to a Private Investigator (PI). It was obvious he needed assistance so the PI asked if he could be of help. With real tears forming in both eyes the young man sadly related that his mother had recently died and he needed to get certified copies of real estate documents so he could settle her estate.

The PI offered his assistance then retrieved and ordered the certified documents for the young man and both went back to the waiting area. The PI (a retired Police Officer) recognized the "Mongols'" tattoo on the young man's neck and asked if he was still a member of the outlaw motorcycle club. He stated in a rough tone "once a member always a member." The PI said he was sorry for the loss of his mother then stated "You know you are going to die too, do you know if you will go to heaven or hell?" The young man responded, "You know you're the third person this week who asked me that same question." The PI told him that their meeting was no accident and that it was by the providence of God that both were in the Recorder's office at that day and time. The PI took out his Bible, turned to the Salvation verses in the book of Romans and was able to lead the young man to the saving grace of Jesus Christ.

As the Christian warrior on the battlefield, or as a military or civilian police officer, the Christian warrior must be as knowledgeable, experienced, qualified, and ready to use his weapon on the spiritual battlefield. The Bible can save lives for all eternity. 1 Peter 3:15 says, "…be ready always to give an answer to every man that asketh you a reason of the hope that is in you with meekness and fear."

- **Seventh**, always be a doer. Everyone who joins the military is trained in a specialty and he must become proficient in every task that is related to that specialty. If the soldier does not meet the minimum standard he may be recycled having to go through the training a second time. Every military specialty has scores of tasks that must be mastered in training and then accomplished on the battlefield. After training, the soldier is assigned to a deployable unit and he will have a team leader within his specialty that ensures he is technically and tactically proficient in performing all assigned tasks timely and correctly. A soldier who does not perform his specialty tasks to standard or does not accomplish additional duties as assigned is counseled and may be reduced in rank. A soldier who does not accomplish assigned tasks on the battlefield may cause serious injury or death to himself or other soldiers and may cause mission failure.

Someone said "those who can - do - and those who can't teach." This does not apply to a soldier. Every soldier must be a doer. He must be able to talk the talk and walk the walk and as he gains experience he becomes a teacher. In the military only the doers become teachers. The professional soldier on the battlefield today does not have to be told by his leader what to do; he knows his duty and responsibilities and performs them as they arise. He is able to accomplish every task and duty without direct supervision because he has already proven his abilities in the classroom and on the training field. General MacArthur said, "Sweat on the training field saves blood on the battlefield."

The infantry soldier has already proven to himself and his leaders that he is a capable and experienced doer. To disable an IED or any other type of explosive takes a soldier who is a fully trained professional dedicated to his specialty, and who is a doer. As an example, there is a retired Air Force service member who has over thirty years experience in Explosive Ordinance Disposal as a technician and instructor with the military and civil law enforcement. As dangerous as this specialty is he once said that it was the best job he ever had. When asked why, he related that his direct supervisor always let him do his job his own way and was never looking over his shoulder telling him what to do. A bomb disposal technician who has earned educational degrees in his specialty and has scored one hundred percent in every written and practical exercise is of no use if he is not a doer on the battlefield.

In the civilian and military education community it is possible to gain academic degrees by classroom, correspondence, or on-line courses. This academic type of education is needed and encouraged in every civilian and military field of study. But, on the battlefield where the bullets are flying and men are dying, battles are fought and won by soldiers who are doers. The combat leader must say to his men, "follow me and do as I do." As an example, in the Army the most highly trained professional infantry combat leaders are those soldiers who wear the Ranger or Special Forces qualification Tab on their left shoulder. Soldiers wearing these Tabs are officers and enlisted men with education degrees from high school to PhD's, and they all have one common factor- they are all doers. Doers, because you cannot earn either of these qualification Tabs by graduating from a college course, correspondence course, on-line course, playing combat video games, or by watching or participating in reality game shows. They are earned by leading by example and leading by doing under the most extreme physical and mental conditions.

A service member who does not do what he is ordered, who does not do what is expected, who does not do what he is asked, who does not do tasks to standard, who does not do what he should do in the absence of orders, will not do in the military service. Every service member must have a "can-do" attitude. The motto of the US Navy Sea Bees is "Can-do." Someone said, "if you think you can you are almost finished, but if you think you can't you have already failed."

The Bible commands the Christian warrior to be a doer also. James 1:23, 25 says, "For if any be a hearer of the word, and not a doer, he is like unto a man beholding his natural face in a glass,...But whoso looketh into the perfect law of liberty, and continueth therein, he being not a forgetful hearer, but a doer of the work, this man shall be blessed in his deed." The word "doer" in these two verses is defined as a person who is a performer, one who obeys or fulfils a duty. A "doer" in Scripture (the manual for the Christian warrior) refers to a mature and experienced Christian. The "doer" in Scripture is always blessed and rewarded.

Joshua tells the Christian to be courageous and "to do" in Joshua 23:6, "Be ye therefore very courageous to keep and to do all that is written in the book…" Christian warriors on the spiritual battlefield are not only called to "talk the talk" but are also called to "walk the walk" and "to do." Just as the soldier must be trained and tested on every task of his specialty the Christian warrior is commanded to do "all" that is written in the book. Not some of the tasks in the book and not most of the tasks, but all that is written. When the soldiers "do" what they are commanded by the word of God they save lives. I Timothy 4:16 says, "Take heed unto thyself, and unto the doctrine, continue in them: for in doing this thou shalt both save thyself, and them that hear thee." When the soldier is attacking or being attacked as he follows military tactical doctrine he will survive, his team will survive and accomplish their mission. The Christian warrior and his team can survive and be victorious on the spiritual battlefield as he follows Biblical doctrine.

The Bible has numerous verses describing promised protection for the Christian warrior who obeys the Word of God, who is faithful to the Word of God and who is a "doer" of the Word of God. The 91st Psalm is only one example: verse 2 says, "the Lord is my refuge and fortress;" verse 3, "he shall deliver thee from the snare;" verse 4, "his truth shall be thy shield;" verse 5, "Thou shalt not be afraid;" verse 7, "A thousand shall fall at thy side, and ten thousand at thy right hand; but it shall not come nigh thee;" verse 9, "the Lord which is my refuge;" verse 11, "For he shall give his angels charge over thee, to keep thee in all thy ways." (The complete 91st Psalm is enclosure #4). A "doer" of the Word and a doer of the Work is courageous and well protected by God so he can survive and accomplish his mission on the spiritual battlefield.

- *Eighth,* be faithful. Faithful is defined as adhering to duty, loyal, true to allegiance, constant in the performance of duties. A faithful person is someone who is observant of all his contracts, vows, oaths, and true to his word. Everyone who enters the military service is required to take this oath of enlistment:

"I, (name), do solemnly swear (or affirm) that I will support and defend the Constitution of the United States against all enemies, foreign and domestic; that I will bear true faith and allegiance to the same; and that I will obey the orders of the President of the United States and the orders of the officers appointed over me, according to regulations and the Uniform Code of Military Justice. So help me God."

A soldier who does not support and defend the United States, who does not bear true faith and allegiance, who does not obey lawful orders is dishonorably discharged from the service.

Soldiers must be faithful to the United States, their service, and to their fellow service members in peace and in time of war. Army soldiers have a creed that they live by and are faithful to:

"I am an American soldier. I am a warrior and member of a team. I serve the people of the United States and live the Army values. I will always place the mission first. I will never accept defeat. I will never quit. I will never leave a fallen comrade. I am disciplined, physically and mentally tough, trained and proficient in my warrior tasks and drills. I always maintain my arms, my equipment and myself. I am an expert and I am a professional. I stand ready to deploy, engage, and destroy the enemies of the United States of America in close combat. I am guardian of freedom and the American way of life. I am an American soldier."

Being a soldier is not just a title-it is not a men and women's social club-it is not a hobby, it is a way of disciplined life on and off the field of battle. Whenever a soldier reports for duty at a new posting or in a combat zone he is giving his life to his unit Commander for the length of time he will serve there. Whatever the commander requests is an "order" that must be accomplished. The request may be to simply sweep and clean up the operations center or to "take that hill." The commander never asks the soldier to think about it, or if he has the time, or to talk to his spouse or men of his squad about it, or to pray about it. It is an order that must be accomplished. Soldiers are expected to risk their life, and the lives of their subordinates for the successful accomplishment of the mission.

The book of Matthew chapter eight gives an example of the faithfulness of Roman soldiers. It tells of a Roman Centurion (a commander of 100 men) who requested Jesus to heal his servant. In verse 7 Jesus says, "I will come and heal him." The Centurion tells Jesus he is not worthy that Jesus should even come into his house and says in verse 8 and 9, "...but speak the word only, and my servant shall be healed. For I am a man under authority, having soldiers under me: and I say to this man, Go, and he goeth; and to another, Come, and he cometh; and to my servant, Do this, and he doeth it." Jesus says in verse 10, "Verily I say unto you, I have not found so great faith, no, not in Israel." The servant was healed because of the faith of the Centurion.

An example of faithfulness to a comrade in arms in Afghanistan can be found in the official narrative of Staff Sergeant Salvatore A. Giunta's Medal of Honor citation which reads in part: "On October 25, 2007 Specialist Giunta's platoon was conducting a movement to contact to interdict enemy forces. His platoon was ambushed by 10 to 15 enemy personnel who utilized an "L" shaped, near ambush that was within 10 meters of the platoon's main body. The enemy fired 10 rocket propelled grenades, 3 machine guns and additional AK-47 automatic weapons which immediately hit and wounded two members of the lead team. While the Squad Leader moved to get a situation report Specialist Giunta provided covering fire by leading his team in suppressing enemy positions, assigning sectors of fire and commanding his M-203 gunner to engage close targets. The Squad Leader was struck in the helmet by an AK-47 round and fell to the ground. Despite being under heavy fire by enemy automatic weapons fire, rocket propelled grenades, and small arms, Specialist Giunta immediately left his covered position in order to render aid to his Squad Leader. Specialist Giunta was struck by two bullets, one struck his armored vest and the other struck a shoulder-launched rocket he was carrying across his back. Recovering from the two impacts he ensured his Squad Leader was not injured and began bounding his fire team forward in an attempt to maneuver on the enemy.

"Specialist Giunta's fire team was pinned down by effective enemy machine gun and small arms fire from multiple positions at close range. Specialist Giunta and team members threw fragmentation grenades and assaulted forward through the enemy positions to where the two members of the lead team were wounded and began treating one. Specialist Giunta realized one member was missing so he continued to push forward along the enemy's exfiltration route, despite taking small arms fire from enemy personnel who were attempting to cover their withdrawal. Moving in the lead and rapidly closing with the enemy, despite receiving effective fire, Specialist Giunta overtook two enemy combatants attempting to drag off the other wounded team member who had been incapacitated by his wounds. Specialist Giunta engaged one enemy combatant at close range and killed him, which caused the other enemy combatant to drop the team member and flee. Specialist Giunta then began immediate first aid and helped his Squad Leader to adjust security, further consolidate casualties, and prepare medical evacuation operations.

"Specialist Giunta's personal courage were the decisive factors in changing the tide of the battle, ensuring that a team member was not captured by the enemy, and preventing the lead fire team from being destroyed by the enemy's near ambush. Despite bullets impacting on and around himself, Specialist Giunta fearlessly advanced on the enemy and provided aid to his fallen comrades. His actions saved the lives of multiple paratroopers and changed the course of the battle in his platoon's favor. Specialist Giunta's extraordinary heroism and selflessness above and beyond the call of duty are in keeping with the highest traditions of military service and reflect great credit upon himself, Company B, 2d Battalion (Airborne), 503d Infantry Regiment, and the United States Army."

After receiving the Medal of Honor Staff Sergeant Giunta stated, "I didn't do anything that any other paratrooper in 1ˢᵗ Platoon, Battle Company, 173ʳᵈ airborne Brigade Combat Team, or anyone in the United States military for that matter, wouldn't have done, and I can't quite understand what all the fuss is about." This is an example of the "faithfulness" a soldier has for his country, for his unit, and for his fellow service members and he expects the same "faithfulness" from every other soldier on today's lethal battlefield.

Every born again Christian is expected to be faithful as God is faithful. Deuteronomy 7:9 says, "Know therefore that the Lord thy God, he is God, the faithful God, which keepeth covenant and mercy with them that love him and keep his commandments to a thousand generations." Every promise God has made to his children He will keep to those who love him and keep His commandments. Soldiers love their country and their service and they take an oath they willingly obey. Christians who accept the gift of salvation from God through his son Jesus Christ are saved by "faith." Ephesians 2:8 says, "For by grace are ye saved through faith; and that not of yourselves: it is the gift of God." Then Romans 10:13 says, "For whosoever shall call upon the name of the Lord shall be saved." As the soldier took an oath, Christians through prayer have called on the Lord to be saved and are committed to faithfully love, serve, and obey the Word of God.

A soldier reveals his love to his country, his commander, and his fellow soldiers by his service and faithfulness to them no matter the circumstances. His love to his wife is demonstrated in the same way, by his actions and faithfulness toward her. Love is an action word, so his actions toward her reveal his love for her. He wants to spend time with her, her family and friends. When a soldier is deployed he calls his wife frequently, or by e-mail, even by the U.S. mail. He is thinking of her when not on missions and is looking forward to his return home.

The Christian reveals his love to his Saviour in the same manner, by his actions and faithfulness. He spends all of his time with Him by calling on his Saviour in prayer at every opportunity. He spends time reading the Bible every day, he wants to spend time with fellow Christians and be in His house (the local church) every time the doors are open, and he looks forward to His return. As a soldier may be called to demonstrate his love toward his fellow soldiers by sacrificing his life for them, the Christian's Saviour has already demonstrated His love. John 3:16 says, "For God so loved the world, that he gave his only begotten Son, that whosoever believeth in him should not perish, but have everlasting life."

As a soldier serves his country and commander, the Christian serves his Commander and country. The words military and service go hand in hand. Everyone has always used the two words interchangeably. A Marine, a Soldier, an Airman, a Sailor, a Guardsman all serve their country. They serve by obeying orders of those Officers and Non-Commissioned Officers who are in positions of authority over them. Soldiers do not always like the duties, tasks, and missions given to them but they always accomplish the duty, task, or mission to the best of their ability because they are always faithful.

The Christian warrior is also required to serve his Commander and country. His commander is his Lord and Saviour Jesus Christ, but the Christian who does live on this world, is not of this world. John 17:14 says, "I have given them thy word; and the world hath hated them, because they are not of the world, even as I am not of the world." The Christian has a heavenly home for all eternity. This is why the Christian is referred to as a stranger, a sojourner, a pilgrim, or an ambassador in Scripture. Psalm 39:12 says, "Hear my prayer, O Lord, and give ear unto my cry; hold not thy peace at my tears: for I am a stranger with thee, and a sojourner, as all my fathers were." I Peter 2:11 says, "Dearly beloved, I beseech you as strangers and pilgrims, abstain from fleshly lusts, which war against the soul," and Ephesians 6:20 says, "For which I am an ambassador in bonds: that therein I may speak boldly, as I ought to speak."

Christians are commanded to serve. Romans 12:1 is just one of numerous verses on Christian service, "I beseech you therefore, brethren, by the mercies of God, that ye present your bodies a living sacrifice, holy, acceptable unto God, which is your reasonable service." A Christian man or woman may have gained experience and education in a specialized field that provides an enjoyable lifestyle, but it does not excuse them from serving their Lord and Saviour in the church of God. Throughout the book of Acts, which gives the history of the local church, people are saved, baptized, and added to the church. Acts 2:41 says, "Then they that gladly received his word were baptized: and the same day there were added unto them about three thousand souls," and verse 47 says "Praising God, and having favour with all the people. And the Lord added to the church daily such as should be saved." Christians are to serve the Lord through the church as the soldier is to serve through the military.

Just as the military provides and trains the soldier in a specialty the Holy Spirit leads the Christian to a local church where his spiritual gift is needed. Upon salvation the new Believer is indwelt by the Holy Spirit who "seals" and "empowers" the believer. Romans 8:9 says in part, "…if so be that the Spirit of God dwell in you…," and Acts 1:8 says, "But ye shall receive power, after that the Holy Ghost is come upon you: and ye shall be witnesses unto me both in Jerusalem, and in all Judaea, and in Samaria, and unto the uttermost part of the earth." Just as the soldier would give his life for his fellow soldiers or to accomplish the mission, Jesus Christ gave his life for the church. Acts 20:28 says, "Take heed therefore unto your selves, and to all the flock, over the which the Holy ghost hath made you overseers, to feed the church of God, which he hath purchased with his own blood."

As the military orders the soldier where to serve, the Holy Spirit directs the Christian where he may serve. Ephesians 4:11-12 says, "And he gave some, apostles; and some, prophets; and some, evangelists; and some, pastors and teachers; For the perfecting of the saints, for the work of the ministry, for the edifying of the body of Christ." A soldier is ordered where to serve in his specialty and the Christian is directed by the Holy Spirit where to serve using his spiritual gifts and natural talents. The Christian is given a triple mission commission in Matthew 28:19-20 which says, "Go ye therefore, and teach all nations, baptizing them in the name of the Father, and of the Son, and of the Holy Ghost: teaching them to observe all things whatsoever I have commanded you: and, lo, I am with you alway, even unto the end of the world. Amen." The Christian is to go and lead sinners to Jesus Christ by giving the gospel; second he's to get them baptized in a local church; and third he's to get the new believer into a discipleship program.

Christians are commanded to obey just as the soldier obeys orders. This command to obey brings a reward to those who are the doers of the command. Job 36:11 says, "If they obey and serve him, they shall spend their days in prosperity, and their years in pleasures." The words obey and obedient are commands to the Christian throughout Scripture. John 14:15 says, "If ye love me, keep my commandments," and Exodus 24:7 says in part, "...and they said, all that the Lord hath said will we do, and be obedient." The purpose of the book of Ecclesiastes is to show man that he should obey the Word of God. The book concludes in chapter 12:13-14 saying "Let us hear the conclusion of the whole matter: Fear God, and keep his commandments: for this is the whole duty of man. For God shall bring every work into judgment, with every secret thing, whether it be good, or whether it be evil."

The soldier's faithfulness is revealed by his love, service, and obedience to his commander just like the Christian's faithfulness to his commander is revealed.

- **Ninth**, never miss a formation. The First Formation in the morning is for the purpose of accounting for every soldier assigned to the unit and to pass out information for the day and upcoming events. The formation is mandatory for every soldier assigned to the unit or company. The unit commander makes announcements that affect each soldier, the unit, and his family. Individual soldiers are often assigned tasks and missions to perform. Therefore, every soldier is attentive and prepared to take note of assignments and tasks assigned to him or his squad. A soldier is either present or accounted for by his immediate leader. At the conclusion of the First Formation the time of the next mandatory formation is announced. A soldier not present for a formation nor accounted for is considered absent without leave (AWOL) and may receive disciplinary action.

As an example, First Formation announcements for an infantry unit may be Army service school dates, the reassignment of personnel into or out of the unit, promotion orders, service school orders, issue of new individual clothing or equipment, weapon qualification information, etc. On occasion volunteers are requested to attend and fill service school vacancies such as Basic Airborne, Jumpmaster school, Pathfinder school, Air Assault school, or Ranger school. Each of these schools are both physically and mentally demanding and require passing the rigorous Army Physical Training Fitness test prior to reporting into the course. Therefore, every soldier in the unit must always be physically fit and ready for deployment.

The Christian warrior, like an infantry soldier, should be in church whenever the doors are open every Sunday morning, Sunday evening, and Wednesday evening for the prayer meeting. He should be present whenever a church meeting or social function is scheduled. He should be in his local church to hear from the man of God, who teaches and preaches from the Word of God, in the house of God. He should also want to hear from their missionary and evangelist whenever he comes to report. The Christian should also be attentive and prepared to take note of assignments and tasks assigned to him. He should be prepared to volunteer for different ministries of the church. He should regard every church service as a mandatory formation.

Every Pastor of a local New Testament church knows each church member and if he is present just as the military commander knows who is AWOL from his formations. The church member who misses a church service or meeting is not disciplined by the pastor but by the Holy Spirit who brings conviction to the born-again believer. The Christian warrior who misses a church service may also miss a directed task or mission by his commander. In the book of Acts 13:1 it describes a regular church service in the city of Antioch and names only a few of the members who were present. Then verse two says, "As they ministered to the Lord, and fasted, the Holy Ghost said, Separate me Barnabas and Saul for the work whereunto I have called them." As you read through the book of Acts you find that Barnabas and Saul become missionaries who preached, got people saved and baptized, and became church planters. God calls men and women today in the same way, not only into the full time ministry, but He also calls church members to serve in the local church.

Another example of the importance of mandatory attendance is found in the Book of John chapter 20. In chapter 19 Jesus was crucified and buried in the tomb. But on Sunday morning, in chapter 20, He was resurrected and first appeared to Mary Magdalene. Later in the evening he appeared where His disciples were assembled for service. In verse 22 Jesus said to them who were assembled, "Receive ye the Holy Ghost." Then verse 24 tells us that Thomas was not with them when Jesus came and he did not believe the resurrection. In verse 25 Thomas says to the disciples who were in attendance, "...except I shall see in his hands the print of the nails, and put my finger into the print of the nails, and thrust my hand into his side, I will not believe," and he has been called "doubting Thomas" ever since. The disciples were together again eight days later and verse 26 tells us, "...and Thomas was with them: then came Jesus..." In verse 27 Jesus says to Thomas, "Reach hither thy finger, and behold my hands; and reach hither thy hand, and thrust it into my side: and be not faithless, but believing." Thomas answered and said unto him, "My Lord and my God."

Any formation may be the soldier's notification of deployment to a combat zone, so every formation is important. Being in church is more important spiritually. The Christian warrior may be called to attend Bible College, into the full time ministry, called as a evangelist or missionary, or called into one of the many ministries of the New Testament church, or to witness a calling. Every church meeting is important and every warrior must be prepared for service and deployment.

- **Tenth**: Be obedient. All military service members are obedient or they would not be in the military. Obedience is mandatory from the lowest private to the most senior General Officer. Every good military leader was and is an obedient follower. Obedient is defined as a person who is submissive to authority, who is in compliance with orders or commands, and who abstains from what is forbidden. Obedience is not a sign of weakness nor is it a lack of self confidence in a soldier; obedience is a sign of trust and faithfulness in those who are in lawfully appointed authority.

A soldier obeys orders he likes and he obeys orders he doesn't like. The soldier's attitude toward the order, the superior giving the order, the circumstances of the order, or the dangers involved in accomplishing the order have absolutely nothing to do with obeying the order. It is an order and all lawful orders must be obeyed. The majority of orders and the rationale for giving them are usually well understood by subordinates. On occasion an order comes down the "chain-of-command" (Division commander, Brigade commander, Battalion commander, Company commander, to Platoon commander) that appears to have no reason for its execution, nor for the expenditure of time, money, personnel, and resources to accomplishment it. When the occasional question of "why" are we doing this comes up a typical military response is, "I don't know the order came from echelons above my pay grade." This translates, only someone at the top of the chain-of-command, at galaxy command headquarters, knows and understands the order. Even though the "why" question was asked for curiosity's sake there was never a doubt of its execution and accomplishment, because soldiers are obedient.

When a U.S. soldier on any battlefield is commanded to "fix bayonets - charge" he does not ask questions, he immediately obeys. He understands fully well what will happen in the next five minutes, he understands the seriousness of the situation, and he puts his trust and faithfulness in the decision of those in authority over him, and he obeys. The 1854 poem by Alfred Lord Tennyson about the Charge of the Light Brigade at the Battle of Balaclava during the Crimean War best sums up a soldiers obedience to orders-"Theirs not to reason why, theirs but to do and die." A soldier does not have to understand the order, only to execute and accomplish the lawful order.

The Christian warrior is also commanded to obey just as the soldier obeys orders. Hebrews 13:17 says, "Obey them that have rule over you, and submit yourselves: for they watch for your souls, as they that must give account, that they may do it with joy, and not with grief: for that is unprofitable for you." Christians are to be law abiding citizens in the cities they live, submitting themselves to local, state, and federal laws. And Titus 3:1 says, "Put them in mind to be subject to principalities and powers, to obey magistrates, to be ready to every good work." Those in lawful authority over the Christian have been placed there by God and are for the protection of His warriors.

This command to obey brings a reward to those who are the doers of the command. Job 36:11 says, "If they obey and serve him, they shall spend their days in prosperity, and their years in pleasures." The words obey and obedient are commands to the Christian throughout Scripture. John 14:15 says, "If ye love me, keep my commandments," and Exodus 24:7 says in part, "...and they said, all that the Lord hath said will we do, and be obedient."

There is a Biblical account of Naaman, who was the commander of the Army of the King of Syria. The Bible says in 2 Kings chapter 5 that he was a great man with his master and honorable and that he was a mighty man in valour, but he was a leper. As a leper, he could not come into contact with anyone, including his immediate family, and could only live with other lepers. In verse 10 of the chapter Naaman is told by the Prophet Elisha to wash in the Jordan River seven times and he would be healed. Naaman had already tried every remedy and probably had spent a fortune on ointments for a cure. When told to wash seven times the Bible says he "was wroth and went away." His subordinates reasoned with him that he did not have to understand the method given by the Prophet of God only to have faith and trust that God would cure him and to obey. Verse 14 concludes by saying, "Then went he down, and dipped himself seven times in Jordan, according to the saying of the man of God: and his flesh came again like unto the flesh of a little child, and he was clean." Naaman's obedience resulted in blessings. Not only blessings to him personally but to the men he served with in the King's army, and to his immediately family. And most importantly, a blessing to God as he could give personal testimony of his cure by his faith and trust in the Word of God and his obedience.

The book of Ecclesiastes, written by King Solomon, reveals his conflict over the problems he observed (and that we see) in life. He goes on to show that man should lead a godly life even though he is not of the world and that man should be obedient to the Word of God. He concludes in chapter 12:13-14 by saying, "Let us hear the conclusion of the whole matter: Fear God, and keep his commandments: for this is the whole duty of man. For God shall bring every work into judgment, with every secret thing, whether it be good, or whether it be evil." Obedience is a mark of a good soldier and of the Christian Warrior.

Battlefield Tactics

"For we wrestle not against flesh and blood, but Against principalities, against powers, against the rulers of the darkness of this world, against spiritual wickedness in high places."

— Ephesians 6:12

As soon as a man or woman accepts Jesus Christ as his Lord and Savior he has enlisted in the Army of God and becomes a warrior on the spiritual battlefield against Satan. Satan knows he can never defeat God so he makes every attempt to cause Christians to fall. The Bible refers to Satan "as a roaring lion…seeking whom he may devour" (1 Peter 5:8). When Satan tried to ascend above God he was thrown from heaven and one third of the angels followed him. These are all Satan's devils and one of their missions is to defeat Christians. This spiritual battle has already been won on the cross by Jesus Christ when he shed his blood and died for sinners and rose again. The Christian has to fight the daily battle against Satan and his fallen angels.

To survive on the battlefield the infantry combat soldier must know everything about his enemy. He must know the uniform he wears, the weapon and his weapons systems, and his tactics. He must know the enemies order of battle, (OB), and he must conduct an Intelligence preparation of the battlefield, (IPB). When this enemy intelligence has been examined, the soldier can plan, prepare, and execute his operation order and be victorious on the battlefield accomplishing his mission.

OB as it pertains to the enemy is knowing how the enemy operates and organizes his forces on the battlefield. The OB factors are composition, disposition, tactics, strength, training, logistics, command and signal, morale, units and personalities. IPB is a systematic, continuous process of analyzing the threat and environment in a specific geographic area of operation. It defines the battlefield environment and its effect on the enemy and friendly forces. After a careful study of both OB and IPB, the enemy's capabilities, vulnerabilities and probable courses of action can be determined. Will the enemy attack, defend, delay, or withdraw?

Satan is our enemy; he is our adversary; he represents the principalities and powers; he is the ruler of the darkness; he is the spiritual wicked one; he is the roaring lion and he is commander of the opposing forces on the spiritual battlefield. And just as the enemy on the unconventional battlefield, he does not identify himself, he wears no standard uniform, he does not follow the Law of Land Warfare, and he does not recognize the Geneva Convention guidelines. Satan is the father of lies (John 8:44(1)), he is the accuser (Revelation 12:10(2)), he is the prince of the devils (Matthew 12:24(3)), he is the prince of the power of the air (Ephesians 2:2(4)), he is the ruler of darkness (Ephesians 6:12(5)), he is the tempter (Matthew 12:43(6)), he is the wicked one (Matthew 13:19(7)), and he is the Christian warrior's enemy (Matthew 13:39(8)). Ephesians 6:11 tells the Christian to "...put on the whole armour of God that ye may be able to stand against the wiles of the devil." The word "wiles" is defined as a trick or stratagem practiced for ensnaring or to deceive. In the context of the verse the word refers to the tactics Satan and his devils use to ensnare and deceive a Christian so he may "devour" him spiritually.

Just as the military leader examines the enemy commander and his forces by conducting in-depth study, let us as Spiritual combat leaders, do likewise of Satan and his devils. The study of our enemy's tactics is necessary for our survival and success on the spiritual battlefield.

First of all, Satan is an angel, a created being. Angels are confirmed one hundred eight times in the Old Testament and one hundred sixty-five times in the New Testament. Jesus personally affirmed their existence numerous times in the Word of God. All angels were created. Colossians 1:16 says, "For by him were all things created, that are in heaven, and that are in earth, visible and invisible..." As personal beings, angels possess the attributes of personality, and they are wise but not all knowing. Matthew 24:36 says, "But of that day and hour knoweth no man, no, not the angels of heaven..." Angels are powerful but not omnipotent. 2 Peter 2:11 says, "Whereas angels, which are greater in power and might...". Angels worship God in Revelation 7:11, "And all the angels stood round about the throne...and worshipped God." Angels are moral beings who have the freedom to obey or disobey. 2 Peter 2:4 says, "For if God spared not the angels that sinned, but cast them down to hell, and delivered them into chains of darkness, to be reserved unto judgment."

Second, Satan is real. Seven Old Testament books and nineteen New Testament books refer to him. Jesus Christ spoke to him, rebuked him, cast out devils, taught about the devil, and defeated him on the cross of Calvary. The name "Satan" means adversary and the name "Devil" means slanderer. Satan is an angel who fell and Isaiah 14:12-17 provides details of his fall. Verse 12 begins by saying, "How art thou fallen from heaven, O Lucifer, son of the morning, how art thou cut down to the ground...." Verse 13 continues by saying, "For thou has said in thine heart, I will ascend into heaven, I will exalt my throne about the stars of God..." Then verses 14-16 relate Satan's wishes and his fall to come, "I will ascend above the heights of the clouds, I will be like the most High. Yet thou shalt be brought down to hell, to the sides of the pit. They that see thee shall narrowly look upon thee, and consider thee, saying, Is this the man that made the earth to tremble, that did shake kingdoms." When Satan fell he convinced other angles to fall with him.

Today Satan is referred to and called the prince of this world in John 12:31(9), 14:30(10), and Ephesians 2:2(11). As the prince, his works are as follows: He claims authority over the world in Luke 4:6, "And the devil said unto him, All this power will I give thee, and the glory of them: for that is delivered unto me; and to whomsoever I will, I give it." He has dominion over and blinds the minds of unbelievers. Acts 26:18 says, "To open their eyes, and to turn them from darkness to light, and from the power of Satan unto God..." and 2 Corinthians 4:4, says "In whom the god of this world hath blinded the minds of them which believe not..." He contends with believers (the saints of God.) Ephesians 6:12 says, "For we wrestle not against flesh and blood, but against principalities, against powers, against the rulers of the darkness of this world, against spiritual wickedness in high places." He slanders the saints. Job 1:11 says, "...put forth thine hand now, and touch all that he hath, and he will curse thee to thy face." He opposes the righteous in Zechariah 3:1, "...Joshua the high priest standing before the angel of the Lord, and Satan standing at his right hand to resist him." He instigates men to sin in John 13:2, "...the devil having now put into the heart of Judas Iscariot, Simon's son, to betray him." And he preys on men in 1 Peter 5:8, "...your adversary the devil, as a roaring lion, walketh about, seeking whom he may devour."

Satan is out to get every soldier on the spiritual battlefield. As a created angel he is not everywhere all at once. He only knows what he can see for himself or what his other fallen angels (devils) tell him. That is why he has to walk about the earth - he is searching for easy prey. Like the enemy on the battlefield he would rather attack and devour spiritual leaders but if he can't he will settle on anyone, maybe a wife or children because they are usually soft targets.

Now that we understand a little more of our enemy, Satan, and his fallen angels, let us examine the spiritual battlefield. The battlefield differs depending where you are living and working. Militarily the battlefield is examined by the intent of the infantry combat commander is he going to attack, defend, delay or withdraw. In the attack the commander looks for terrain or obstacles that will mask the movement of his forces, but at the same time provide easy and quick avenues of approach as they close the distance to destroy the enemy. Conversely, in the defense the commander looks for terrain and obstacles that will conceal his forces from enemy observation and at the same time provide protective cover from enemy weapon systems; and that will greatly hinder the movement of enemy forces toward his position. For the defense the commander also searches for terrain that will naturally channel the movement of enemy forces into a kill zone. If a natural channel is not available the commander will place barriers such as anti-personnel and anti-tank mines that will force the enemy into a kill zone. Every avenue of escape out of the kill zone will be covered by direct and indirect fire to destroy fleeing enemy forces.

If the battlefield is in a built-up area such as a small town or large metropolitan city the tactics to attack, defend, delay, or withdraw are much different but the principles remain the same. For the purpose of this chapter we will focus on the tactics used by Satan and his fallen angels toward individuals and small groups such as families and churches.

Scripture gives numerous warnings to the Christian warrior regarding who and what to look out for on the battlefield. These are excellent examples of soft targets Satan looks for:

- Luke 12:15, "…Take heed, and beware of covetousness: for a man's life consisteth not in the abundance of the things which he possesseth." Covetousness is a strong or inordinate desire of obtaining and possessing some supposed good, or an inordinate desire of wealth. Satan will entice a person to covet for wealth or possessions that are out of his immediate reach. 1 Corinthians 7:5 says, "...that Satan tempt you not..." and when man is in sin he can tempt himself with his own lust and covetousness. James 1:14 says, "But every man is tempted, when he is drawn away of his own lust, and enticed."

- Philippians 3:2, "Beware of dogs, beware of evil workers..." The word "dogs" here refers to the evil workers who entice Christians into sin and false teachings.

- Colossians 2:8, "Beware lest any man spoil you through philosophy and vain deceit, after the tradition of men, after the rudiments of the world, and not after Christ." Evil men can spoil or corrupt a Christian by teaching a false philosophy that changes with society; or a teaching that is based on a tradition, practice, or custom based on man not on the Word of God.

- 2 Peter 3:17, "...beware lest ye also, being led away with the error of the wicked, fall from your own steadfastness" and Matthew 24:4 says, "And Jesus answered and said unto them, Take heed that no man deceive you." The best defense against these evil and wicked men is to stay in the manual and continue in the book which is the Holy Bible.

The Bible also commands the Christian warrior to "take heed." The word "heed" is defined as: to give mind to or regard with care, to take notice of or to give attention to a danger, to observe with caution, to be vigilant and circumspect, or to guard against danger.

- Mark 4:24, "And he said unto them, Take heed what ye hear: with what measure ye mete, it shall be measured to you: and unto you that hear shall more be given."

- Luke 21:8, "And he said, Take heed that ye be not deceived: for many shall come in my name, saying, I am Christ; and the time draweth near: go ye not therefore after them."

- I Corinthians 10:12, "Wherefore let him that thinketh he standeth take heed lest he fall."

- I Timothy 4:16, "Take heed unto thyself, and unto the doctrine; continue in them: for in doing this thou shalt both save thyself, and them that hear thee."

The Christian warrior manual warns him to be careful of what he hears and who he hears it from so he will not be deceived. There are many evil wicked men and women who attempt to deceive. The book of Proverbs warns who to watch out for:

- 1:10 warns, "My son, if sinners entice thee, consent thou not."

- 1:15 warns, "...walk not thou in the way with them."

- 4:14 warns, "Enter not into the path of the wicked, and go not in the way of evil men."

- 6:17-19 warns, "A proud look, a lying tongue, and hands that shed innocent blood, A heart that deviseth wicked imaginations, feet that be swift in running to mischief, A false witness that speaketh lies, and he that soweth discord among brethren."

- 7:5 warns, "...keep thee from the strange woman, from the stranger which flattereth with her words."

- 7:27 sums up the harlot by warning, "Her house is the way to hell, going down to the chambers of death."

A wicked man is anyone who deviates from the Word of God, a person who is addicted to vice and who is immoral, a person who lives in sin and is unreconciled to God. An evil man is a person who deviates from moral rules of conduct prescribed by God (sin), or by legitimate human authority (crime), or who violates the plain principles of justice and rectitude. These men are depraved, have a corrupted heart, and are disposed to commit wickedness.

The Bible describes the wicked man's actions in Mark 7:21-23 which says, "For from within, out of the heart of men, proceed evil thoughts, adulteries, fornications, murders, thefts, covetousness, wickedness, deceit, lasciviousness, an evil eye, blasphemy, pride, foolishness: All these evil things come from within, and defile the man." Let's further define the actions of men the Christian warrior should avoid:

- Adulteries - Sexual intercourse with any married woman not his wife.

- Fornications - the lewdness of unmarried persons having sexual intercourse with one another.

- Murders - the act of unlawfully killing a human being with premeditated malice.

- Thefts - to steal or to privately deprive the owner of property against his will.

- Covetousness - a strong desire of obtaining and possessing some supposed good, an inordinate desire of wealth.

- Wickedness - the evil practices of immorality, crime, sin, corrupt manners, or a departure from the rules of divine law.

- Deceit - the leading of another person to believe what is false, or not to believe what is true, to ensnare or cheat.

- Lasciviousness - an irregular indulgence of animal desires, wantonness, lustfulness, to excite lust.

- Evil eye - looking to promote or produce mischief that is wicked, corrupt, or perverse.

- Blasphemy - an injury toward God by denying that which is due and belonging to him, by words or writing.

- Pride - inordinate self-esteem, unreasonable conceit of one's own superiority in talents, beauty, wealth, accomplishments, rank or elevation in office, in contempt of others.

- Foolishness - a person who is destitute of reason and understanding, deficient in intellect (but not an idiot), a course contrary to the dictates of wisdom.

The Christian warrior also has to watch for his own sinful lusts. 1 John 2:16 says, "For all that is in the world, the lust of the flesh, and the lust of the eyes, and the pride of life, is not of the Father, but is of the world." The lust of the flesh refers to physical desires, the lust of the eyes refers to personal desires, and the pride of life refers to self-interests.

The warrior manual also tells the Christian how to check what people say is truth. Acts 17:10-11 tells us of the men of the Berean church that, "…they received the word with all readiness of mind, and searched the scriptures daily, whether those things were so." And Psalm 119:11 says, "Thy word have I hid in mine heart, that I might not sin against thee." Just as the infantry warrior relies on his manuals for his survival on the battlefield the Christian warrior must depend on the Word of God for his survival on the spiritual battlefield.

Satan is the enemy and he is in our neighborhood, our school, and our workplace and these areas are where the spiritual battles take place. Here are only a few of his tactics:

- Tactic #1. We have already discussed the importance of being a "hard target" and what that entails. The soldier on today's lethal battlefield has been well trained and is well versed in this by his combat experience. The leader of the household must also make himself a hard target on the spiritual battlefield. If that leader is also a military combat veteran he has the experience necessary to survive and win on that battlefield. Satan uses the identical tactic as the enemy on the unconventional battlefield who attempts to capture or kill those in leadership positions. He will attack the leader of the household possibly causing the family to turn away from God and his church.

Satan is physically unable to kill a Christian. This has been proven in the book of Job. In chapter one of Job, Satan comes before God and God asks him where he has been. Satan says in verse 7, "...From going to and fro in the earth, and from walking up and down in it." God then asks if Satan has considered Job by stating in verse 8, "...there is none like him in the earth, a perfect and an upright man, one that feareth God, and eschewed evil?" Satan's response is that Job has had everything given to him by God who has protected him from all evil and that if God took it all away "he will curse thee to thy face." In verse 12 God replies to Satan, "...Behold, all that he hath is in thy power; only upon himself put not forth thine hand..." As you read the rest of the Book you find that Job suffered greatly from the "wiles" of Satan but Job never cursed God and Satan could not take his life.

Satan will cause the leader to become missing in action or wounded in action and unable to lead his family. Or he will cause the family to lose confidence and respect in the father and husband, and they will no longer listen to his commands and counsel. When a leader is out of the way the team or unit is temporarily (maybe permanently) disorganized and possibly unable to accomplish their mission. Satan will use whatever "lust" the leader is susceptible to that will cause him to fall in the eyes of his family. Just as the enemy on the unconventional battlefield knows the weaknesses of the American soldier, Satan knows the weaknesses of the Christian family leader and what will cause him to fail and fall.

- Tactic #2. When Satan is unable to capture or kill the family leader he will settle for the spouse or the children for they are the "soft" target. The combat leader is responsible for all of his men, for their training and for their success on the battlefield and mission accomplishment. The Christian leader is also responsible for his family's training and success on the spiritual battlefield and mission accomplishment.

As the combat leader ensures each team member is properly equipped, properly trained in his specialty and fully briefed on his mission, the Christian leader has the identical responsibility to each family member. He must ensure each family member is putting on the full armor of God each day and is prepared for the spiritual battlefield. Combat team members are proficient in at least one other team specialty so they can replace another soldier who is missing in action, wounded in action, or killed in action. The assistant team leader is also prepared to replace the Team leader should the need arise so that whatever occurs throughout the day or week mission accomplishment will not be jeopardized. The Christian leader must ensure each family member becomes a hard target.

- Tactic #3. Creates danger areas. The Army defines a danger area as any place where the leaders estimate tells him that his men might be exposed to enemy observation, fire, or both. When an Army unit finds it necessary to cross a danger area, the unit does so with great caution and as quickly as possible. A danger area may be any open area, a cross road or trail, any village-town-or city, a minefield, stream, or wire obstacle. There are specific tactical procedures to move across each type of danger area. The combat leader is responsible to train his men so they may cross the danger area quickly and safely so they may continue with mission execution and accomplishment.

Prior to deployment into a combat zone, soldiers receive extensive briefings and training on enemy tactics. One enemy tactic concerns the "lust of the eyes." Soldiers on the battlefield often want to pick up a souvenir to bring back home. It could be an enemy weapon, piece of equipment, flag or banner, uniform, etc. Many of these items left in the open for U.S. soldiers to easily see are "booby trapped" and can cause great bodily injury or death to the soldier and those near him. The Christian warrior must look out for these same tactics on the spiritual battlefield. Satan knows what is attractive to men, women, and their children so he booby traps these items to cause spiritual injury. Proverb 7 provides excellent descriptions of his entrapped prey. Verse 22-23 says, "...as an ox goeth to the slaughter, or as a fool to the correction of the stocks; Till a dart strike through his liver; as a bird hasteth to the snare, and knoweth not that it is for his life."

The Christian warrior is also responsible to identify danger areas on the spiritual battlefield and to train all family members so they may cross them quickly and safely. An often used tactic for Satan is to use any sinful lust that an individual engaged in prior to his salvation. Therefore, danger areas on the spiritual battlefield will be different for the leader and for each member of the family. Possible examples may be:

- Husband danger areas: Anywhere alcoholic beverages are served, prescription drugs, casinos or any gambling location, prostitution "red light" districts and/or massage parlors, homosexual districts, pornographic sites or selling locations, the internet, and so called friends and associates who continue to engage in sinful lusts of the flesh, of the eyes, or the pride of life, etc.

- The workplace and old friends are especially a danger to the new Christian who has been born again. 2 Corinthians 5:17 says, "Therefore if any man be in Christ, he is a new creature: old things are passed away; behold, all things are become new." This means he is a new person who has been cleansed by the blood of the Lamb. All sin has been forgiven and he has become a babe in Christ. Co-workers, friends and relatives will see a change and may not like it. They will do everything they can to get him to return to his old ways: whatever that was, going back to sex, drugs, and rock and roll, back to alcohol, back to pornography, back to stealing from your employer, back to gambling, back to lying, etc. They will want the "old" man back not the "new creature". Satan will use everyone he can to get him back into sin. It is a choice the new Christian must make, to return to the old man he was, or to remain faithful to the Word of God. The Holy Spirit will empower him to make the right choice. John 1:12 says, "But as many as received him, to them gave he power to become the sons of God, even to them that believe on his name."

- Wife danger areas: Same as the husband in many areas and socializing with gossips, spending too much time and money in shopping malls, and as the husband, those friends and associates who continue to lust in their areas of weakness, etc.

- Child danger areas: All children are special soft targets for Satan. Children should never be alone in public as they are preyed upon by men, women and even older children of both sexes. Parents should always have physical control, social control, educational control, and emotional control of their children as they are directed by Scripture in Ephesians 6:4 which says, "And, ye fathers, provoke not your children to wrath: but bring them up in the nurture and admonition of the Lord."

In Afghanistan the enemy (Taliban) gives a $25,000 (U.S.) reward to any Afghan national for the capture or killing of a U.S. soldier, or $25,000 to the family of a suicide bomber when a U.S. soldier is killed. Where $70.00 (U.S.) is considered a good monthly wage $25,000 is like becoming a millionaire. Every U.S. soldier outside the "wire" has to take precaution against reward seeking civilians. A few years ago, two U.S. Special Forces soldiers were in their HUMVEE driving through the busy city of Kabul, Afghanistan. It was during the day and many local people were out and the streets were filled with pedestrians, civilian vehicles, public buses, commercial jingle trucks, bicycles, horses, donkey carts, and the usual animals (sheep, goats, camels, donkeys.) There are no rules of the road in Afghanistan, so the streets and sidewalks were all filled with all this traffic going in every direction with no traffic control. It was another extremely hot summer day as they drove through the mass of stop and go vehicle and pedestrian traffic with their windows down letting in the little breeze there was. A pedestrian walked past their slow moving vehicle, raised his hand and dropped a grenade into the HUMVEE. The grenade exploded, miraculously not killing either soldier. One of the soldiers was a Special Forces qualified medic who immediately called for the "Quick Reaction Force," treated himself and the more seriously wounded driver, and both survived.

This tactic is typical of the enemy on the unconventional battlefield. Waiting until the U.S. soldier is tired, bored, in a routine and not expecting enemy contact - then he strikes. The enemy mingles among innocent civilians then strikes out when least expected and is able to blend in with the local population to escape. Satan is even more inventive and lethal.

On another day two unarmed American NGO (non-government organization) employees were shopping at a busy market place on "Chicken Street" in Kabul, Afghanistan. It was another hot summer day and the market place was filled with thousands of local civilian shoppers. As the Americans walked past numerous parked bicycles one of them blew up killing the two Americans and several Afghans and seriously wounded many Afghanistan civilians. The Americans had been followed and the bicycle placed where they would pass by so the explosive could be command detonated as they passed. Knowing the American military Quick Reaction Force and Afghan Army would come immediately to render aid, a second bicycle bomb exploded killing U.S. military personnel and Afghan military and local civilians. The enemy is not concerned how many of his own civilians are killed or wounded as long as an American is killed or wounded so they may get the reward. The enemy on the unconventional battlefield is ruthless, heartless and lethal, just as ruthless, heartless and lethal as Satan on the spiritual battlefield.

In 2005, also in Afghanistan, a Special Forces "A" team was on a mission to capture a known Taliban leader. He lived in a typical high walled, multi-family compound. The team was inserted at night by helicopter into the compound and team members immediately began searching each room for the enemy leader. As team members entered one of the bedrooms, the enemy leader was pointing an AK-47 at the door as he crouched behind his wife and children using them as protection. The first two team members who entered the bedroom hesitated only for a second not wanting to kill or injure the unarmed family members. Both Sergeants were killed in action and the Taliban leader was killed by other team members. This is also typical of the enemy on the unconventional battlefield. They have no compassion for anyone and will use whatever tactic is necessary to survive and further their cause. Satan also has no compassion and will use anyone and anything to cause a Christian warrior to fall.

Just as combat soldiers on the unconventional battlefield prepare themselves mentally and physically, ready their weapons and put on their body armor whenever they leave camp (outside the wire), the Christian warrior should do likewise for his entire family. When the family or an individual family member leaves the home to visit friends, relatives, sporting events, the movies, out to dinner, the mall, etc., he should consider himself in a danger area and take the necessary precautions. Satan will use old friends, co-workers, relatives, and neighbors in every location, and use every seductive lure to entice the Christian to fall. John 15:19 says, "If ye were of the world, the world would love his own: but because ye are not of the world, but I have chosen you out of the world, therefore the world hateth you."

The combat leader knows the strengths and weaknesses of each of his soldiers, what they are capable of, who can work unsupervised, and who can be depended upon in times of stress and emergency. He also knows what danger areas each soldier is susceptible to. It is the combat leader who is fully responsible for each of his soldiers individually and as a team or unit in their conduct on the unconventional battlefield and mission accomplishment. He is responsible for all the team or unit accomplishes or fails to accomplish. The Christian leader of the family has the identical responsibility and should know each family member in as much, if not more, detail.

We have talked at some length about danger areas, but let's identify areas on the unconventional battlefield where a soldier is safe. As we have already discussed there are no battle lines so the enemy is everywhere on the battlefield. The only safe place is where the U.S. has concentrated soldiers, weapons and weapon systems and equipment. In Afghanistan and Iraq the U.S. has built heavily fortified compounds or camps, placed guards at every point of entry, and have gun emplacements at every strategic location that will cover all enemy avenues of approach. Each compound or camp is situated so they can provide mutual support to each other in case of attack and there are always supporting aircraft and artillery. Inside the compound, soldiers sleep in tents or huts which are surrounded by sand bags or concrete barriers. All soldier recreation areas, dining facilities, theaters, etc., are also surrounded by the same type of barriers. Every soldier also has been assigned a "station" to man when and if the enemy should attack the compound.

Everything imaginable is done to safeguard soldiers and military equipment, but the enemy still gets in. The enemy is able to shoot indirect fire weapons into the compound such as rockets, mortars, RPG's (rocket propelled grenades), etc. Most of these types of weapons are not accurate and the enemy is not properly trained or skilled in their employment. The enemy also makes every attempt to surreptitiously enter into the compound by wearing Afghan Army uniforms, as an Afghan civilian worker within the compound, or by climbing over the barriers. If successful the enemy has access to most open areas and can easily kill soldiers or destroy military equipment and aircraft. Even in these so called safe areas the U.S. combat soldier is still required to have immediate access to his personal weapon for his self defense.

Another safe area for the U.S. soldier is another camp or compound. U.S. camps are located throughout the country whereever the enemy is concentrated. U.S. allies in Iraq and Afghanistan have also built fortified camps for their soldiers. When soldiers go outside the wire on a convoy mission, possibly taking needed supplies and/or equipment to another U.S. camp, and if attacked they may enter an allied camp for support or medical assistance. All U.S. and allied camp locations are identified and located and phone numbers and radio frequencies are kept for emergencies. The safest area on the unconventional battlefield is inside a U.S. or allied camp.

The Christian warrior on the spiritual battlefield should be just as careful in the selection of safe areas for himself and his family. It is the combat leader's responsibility to make his home safe. You must throw out anything that is unsafe in your home. You would not keep a five gallon can of gasoline in the home, so why would you let a teenage girl have a computer in her bedroom with uncontrolled, unsupervised access to the web? Just as the can of gasoline is life threatening, the web is dangerous spiritually. Look for IED's in the home and remove them. Satan makes them look appealing and seductive to every member of the family. Just as a new soldier assigned to the team or squad needs close supervision for his survival on the battlefield, children need the same supervision spiritually.

As the leader of the home we must be careful who we invite into the home. We would not let a stranger into our home under a pretext of a home inspection, etc., unless we had coordinated with a company in advance and have an appointed day and time. Any other stranger who enters may return to burglarize or commit any other felony when we are away. We must be just as diligent and careful about who comes into the home as so called "friends." Even friends who profess to be Christians are not always Christians. In Matthew chapter seven Jesus Christ is telling us about those who profess to know him and in verse 22-23 He says, "Many will say to me in that day, Lord, Lord, have we not prophesied in thy name? and in thy name have cast out devils? And in thy name done many wonderful works? And then will I profess unto them, I never knew you: depart from me, ye that work iniquity."

A Christian home is a home where it is known that all family members have accepted Jesus Christ as their Lord and Saviour; a home where the entire family not only professes Christ as their Saviour but faithfully attends a local church each Sunday. Just as another U.S. or allied forti-fied camp is a safe area for the combat soldier another Christian home can be considered a safe area. And the leader of the home is just as dili-gent, and careful as we are who come into the home. It is the combat leader's responsibility for "force protection" inside the camp or com-pound on the unconventional battlefield. And it is the husband and father's responsibility to safeguard the home, not the wife. We would not let an untrained spouse be responsible for "force protection" on the battlefield.

Another safe area on the spiritual battlefield is your home church. It is the house of God, where you hear the Word of God from your preacher – a man of God. Your local church belongs to Jesus Christ who gave His life for it and has stated that nothing shall prevail against it. We as church members, the pastor and deacons have to make the church safe. If we should see a potential IED within the church such as a gossip, or a practicing alcoholic, or a user of illegal drugs, or a pornographic "favorite" site on a church computer, we should do as soldiers on the battlefield-call in the EOD (explosive ordinance disposal) expert. In the church this expert is the pastor and deacons. Just as the enemy on the battlefield is doing, the spiritual enemy is always attempting to infiltrate into all safe areas where he can attack you and your family, in the home and in the church. 2 Peter 2:1 warns, "But there were false prophets also among the people, even as there shall be false teachers among you, who privily shall bring in damnable heresies, even denying the Lord that bought them, and bring upon themselves swift destruction."

- Tactic #4. Sets Improvised Explosives Devices (IED's). IED's are nonstandard explosive devices used to target U.S. soldiers and civilians. The purpose is to instill fear and diminish U.S. resolve on the unconventional battlefield with mounting casualties. IED's can be detonated by remote control as by the ring of a cell phone, or by the combination of wire and a power source or timed fuse. They can also be detonated after being dropped, thrown, or impacted in some manner. An IED can vary from the size of a ballpoint pen to the size of a water heater. They are most often contained in innocent looking objects to camouflage their true purpose. IED vests are worn by suicide bombers (of all ages and sexes) who will approach a soldier or group of soldiers then self-detonate.

Combat leaders receive extensive countermeasure training in regard to the IED threat on the lethal battlefield. This training consists of:

- Ensuring all-round security at all times. Soldiers must scan rooftops and bridge overpasses for enemy activity.

- Convoy security: Vehicles should always travel in convoys, vary their road speed, all occupants of the vehicle should have their weapons pointed in an alert and defensive posture and scan their area of observation.

- Turns: Avoid moving toward or stopping for an item in the roadway.

- Audible signals: Be aware of flares, gunfire, lights, horns honking which can be used to signal the approach of a convoy.

- Enemy observers: Be alert for people who seem overly interested in your convoy, especially those using cell phones while watching your convoy.

- Unusual silence: Often times the local civilians have been warned of an enemy attack on U.S. forces.

- Souvenirs: Do not pick up war trophies or souvenirs as they may be booby trapped. Any item that is seductive to the U.S. soldier and just laying about is probably an IED.

This short list of subjects is only a small portion of the hands-on training given combat leaders prior to deployment to the unconventional battlefield. The Christian warrior on the spiritual battlefield should be just as well trained to identify IED's and how to employ countermeasures for the protection of himself and his family. Satan sets IED's for the same purpose-to instill fear and diminish a Christian's resolve on the spiritual battlefield and in the home. He will do anything to make the leader of the family become an MIA, WIA, or KIA. If he can spiritually defeat the leader, the rest of the family, if not properly trained, will soon fall and also become a casualty. Satan is highly skilled to camouflage his IED's so they are attractive and seductive to not only the family leader but to every member of the family team. Here are just a few IED's that Satan places in your home:

- IED #1. The television. Would you let a young couple come into your home, sit on your couch, then watch them kiss passionately, undress and have sex with your entire family watching? Of course not, but that is happening on almost every channel every evening in every home. If not actually having sex, then they are talking about it. This behavior is so typical today that most people are so accustomed to it that it is routine. Jeremiah 6:15 says, "Were they ashamed when they had committed abomination? Nay, they were not at all ashamed, neither could they blush: therefore they shall fall among them that fall: at the time that I visit them they shall be cast down, saith the Lord." Do not let Satan accustom you or your family to evil abominations.

Television today is attacking family values. If you are old enough you may remember TV programs such as the Nelson family, Father knows best, Leave it to Beaver, or Andy Griffith. These programs contained a moral message to the entire family. Today's programs like the Simpsons, or Married with Children, always have the father or husband portrayed as a moron and unable to lead or control the family. Today even the title "Father knows best" could never be aired.

If you have children you are encouraged to monitor everything that is being watched. If a TV program is not suitable for your children then it probably is not suitable for you. Television should not be used as a babysitter. TV movies and commercials are attempting to re-program and change societal values. If you are not able to monitor everything that is being watched because of work or school schedules then give the TV away. The television is an IED booby trap that Satan has placed inside your home and it is as deadly spiritually as the AK-47.

- IED #2. The internet. When you or your children go onto the web searching for a particular specific subject what often pops up is some type of introduction to a pornographic site. Something will flash which attracts your attention to it and you are encouraged to "click on it." It is so easy to do-one little click and you're there, or your children are there. And you are not even searching for pornography. Satan, the enemy, will use whatever device, lure, or trick it takes to get you to click on it. Sometimes all it takes is a look. Remember the verse in I John 2:16, "For all that is in the world, the lust of the flesh, and the lust of the eyes, and the pride of life, is not of the Father, but is of the world." When you see something seductive to your senses all it takes is a quick look and the idea takes shape in your mind and you begin to lust after it. The best defense is not to look. Never put yourself into a position or location where you may be tempted.

Another internet IED is "chat rooms" etc., where you, your spouse or children may begin chatting with an unknown person that leads to some type of relationship. It may appear to be innocent at first but the individual (enemy) on the other end has a goal in mind- sexual seduction. He (usually a male) or she will, in time, attempt to make personal contact. Sexual predators are on the net searching every hour of every day for a victim. Some have been able to talk teenaged girls to get on a plane or bus to meet them.

Computers and the web are an important communication and education tool today but a parent must monitor who, what, where, when, how, and why the child is on any particular site. Husbands, wives, fathers and mothers must monitor and approve each site, and never allow a child to have an e-mail address that you do not have access to. Husbands and wives should do likewise. There are many web "blockers" that are available to assist you in safeguarding you and your family. It is possible for parents to "sync" all family computers so every member of the family knows who is using each computer and what site they are on. This safeguard keeps each family member accountable.

A soldier on the battlefield would never, ever, put himself in a position that would expose him or his team to enemy direct or in-direct fire. The Christian warrior on the spiritual battlefield must take the same precautions.

- IED # 3. The radio, talk shows and music. There are many crude talk show hosts (that is what they call themselves) who can influence your family. After listening for hours and then days we become desensitized to the foul language and subjects. It is the same with music that is listened to. The words can be crude and the message of the song can be obscene. Just as the TV, we can become desensitized to the point of becoming unable to be "ashamed and not able to blush" as stated in Jeremiah 6:15. For this reason be extremely careful what radio stations and music you and your family listen to.

During WWII the enemy used to broadcast American music to U.S. soldiers in attempts to influence them to surrender. They used female broadcasters with names such as Tokyo Rose. In Viet Nam the name was Hanoi Hanna. Between songs these women told soldiers that the U.S. was losing the war and they may as well surrender, that civilians back home were against the war, that their wives and girlfriends were leaving them and would not be waiting for them on their return, etc. These attempts were not successful but Satan is a master at broadcasting what is needed to cause a Christian warrior to fall. He uses TV, radio and the internet to get his message down to every soldier on the spiritual battlefield. The best countermeasure is not to watch, not to enter the wrong internet site, and not to listen to Satan's broadcasts.

- IED #4. Friend or Foe. On the battlefield soldiers are trained to determine who is a friend or a foe. A soldier has to be constantly on-guard for the enemy. You never know when he will come, or how he will come. On the conventional battlefield the enemy will make every attempt to get "behind the lines" so he can create havoc, cause confusion, destroy equipment or kill soldiers; on the unconventional battlefield (no battle lines) the enemy will make every attempt to get into your camp, base or home for the same purpose.

The soldier on guard duty has a grave responsibility for the protection of fellow soldiers and equipment. He is trained how to set up a guard station, how to set up booby traps and antipersonnel mines, how to camouflage himself so he won't be seen by the enemy, how to use night vision devices, and how to challenge an individual attempting to get past the lines or into the camp. Let us look at an example of an individual attempting to get into a camp at night. The guard should already know that a friendly team or squad is to be expected within a specified time frame. Prior to approaching the guard site the team or squad leader would radio the guard that he is near his position. As the individual nears the guard site the soldier challenges him by the statement, "Halt, who goes there, friend or foe?" The answer is "friend" and the guard then orders the individual to come forward and close enough to be heard by only one another. Then the guard gives the password challenge of (example) "Who is Mickey Mouse's best friend?" The response would be (example) "Rin-Tin-Tin." The correct response would never be the obvious actual friend. After the correct response the guard orders the individual to come forward to be recognized and he then gives another challenge stating the number 3, the individual should respond with the number 6, if the combination password of numbers total 9 (example). The guard would then ask the fellow soldier if he is by himself or with others. If there are others the guard would ask how many, then have the individual stand by him as the individual identifies each soldier by name as the correct number pass by.

How do you and your family choose friends? The Christian warrior must be as careful in the selection of friends as the soldier on the battlefield. Remember this "friend" may look like a sheep but in reality he may be a wolf. What are your challenges and passwords? If the enemy gets behind your lines and into your home, he will cause as much havoc, confusion and destruction as the enemy.

A friend is a person who is attached to you by affection, he has esteem and respect for you and desires your company, and he wants to promote happiness and prosperity to you and your entire family. The friend of a Christian warrior must be another Christian warrior. I Peter 1:15 says, "But as he which hath called you is holy, so be ye holy in all manner of conversation, because it is written, Be ye holy; for I am holy." In Scripture the word "holy" means to be set apart for a sacred purpose and the word "conversation" refers to a person's lifestyle and behavior. Christians are different from the rest of the world. I Peter 2:9-10 says, "But ye are a chosen generation, a royal priesthood, an holy nation, a peculiar people; that ye should shew forth the praises of him who hath called you out of darkness into marvelous light: Which in time past were not a people, but are now the people of God: which had not obtained mercy, but now have obtained mercy."

The enemy of the Christian warrior is: Any person who is against the Biblical standard of purity; any person who does and encourages us to do things that the Bible tells us we should not do; a person who does things that are harmful to our bodies; a person who wants to harm other people; a person who stops or hinders us from doing our duty; a person who interferes with our walk with Jesus Christ. These people are our enemies, not our friends. They are the people God wants us to separate ourselves from because we have nothing in common with them. 2 Corinthians 6:17 says, "Wherefore come out from among them, and be ye separate, saith the Lord, and touch not the unclean thing: and I will receive you."

Wounded in Action - Missing in Action - Killed in Action

"But God commendeth his love toward us, in that, while we were yet sinners, Christ died for us."

— Romans 5:8

Wounded, missing and killed in action are frightening military terms. They are frightening for the soldier, his family and friends. Missing in action is defined as a soldier who has been surrounded or captured by a hostile force who prevents his escape and his location is unknown. Wounded in action is defined as a soldier who has received an injury due to enemy hostile actions, whether by a piercing of the body, fracture, burn, blast concussions, or biological and chemical warfare agents. Killed in action is defined as a soldier who is killed outright or who dies as a result of wounds or other injuries before reaching a medical treatment facility. The term "action" refers to the conduct of combat operations against a hostile enemy force.

The Christian warrior may become WIA, MIA, or KIA on the spiritual battlefield as a result of sin in his life. Sin is any action or inaction that is contrary to the Word of God. When a Christian sins he must confess the sin, repent of the sin, then pray for forgiveness. First John

1:9 says, "If we confess our sins, he is faithful and just to forgive us our sins, and to cleanse us from all unrighteousness." The born-again warrior becomes "wounded in action" when he falls into sin that not only controls his behavior but it stops him from confessing, repenting, and praying for forgiveness. Sin can be pleasurable for a limited time which would hinder the Christian from immediately asking forgiveness. Hebrews 11:25 says, "Choosing rather to suffer affliction with the people of God, than to enjoy the pleasures of sin for a season." When the Christian warrior repents and asks for forgiveness he immediately becomes righteous again but he must still pay the consequences of the sin.

The consequence of living a sinful life will cause wounds to the sinner, his family and friends. The wound may not be serious, somewhat serious, or very serious; and it may affect the sinner, his family and friends in each category. Many people who acknowledge pleasurable sin in their life often say "It's my life, it's my body, and I'm not hurting anyone." But Scripture says different. The book of Joshua chapters six and seven teaches about an Israel soldier whose sin was imputed to the entire nation. The first city Israel defeated as they entered into the Promised Land was Jericho. In Joshua 6:19 God tells Israel what to do with the spoils of war when He says, "But all the silver, and gold, and vessels of brass and iron, are consecrated unto the Lord: they shall come into the treasury of the Lord." Achan took 200 shekels of silver, a Babylonian garment and a wedge of gold weighing 50 shekels and buried them in his tent. As a result he, his wife and children were stoned to death for violating the ban against keeping the spoils of war. Then the Army of Israel was defeated in the battle against Ai, losing thirty-six men as a result of Achan's sin. The sin of one selfish Israel warrior caused "wounds" and death to himself, his family and to the nation Israel.

A soldier on the battlefield may think because of the fog of war and the sounds and confusion of battle that his sin will not be revealed.

There have been numerous accounts and criminal charges against U.S. servicemen in Iraq, Afghanistan and in Cuba who have abused enemy prisoners, embezzled government funds, raped civilian and U.S. service women, abused authority, and who have killed civilian non-combatants. Sin can never be hidden. The Bible says in Numbers 32:23, "But if ye will not do so, behold, ye have sinned against the Lord: and be sure your sin will find you out."

Just as the physical "wounds" of war scar a soldier for his lifetime the wounds of the spiritual battlefield may scar the sinner, his family and friends for a lifetime. For example, sin that ends a marriage in divorce wounds the immediate family and friends but it also wounds the next generation of the family.

A soldier on the battlefield may be discharged from the service because of his sinful actions and if found guilty of criminal charges he could have from administrative disciplinary actions to serving a federal prison sentence as a result. The Christian warrior will also have consequences to serve, but he will never lose his salvation nor be discharged from the family of God. Jesus says in John 10:27-29, "My sheep hear my voice, and I know them, and they follow me: And I give unto them eternal life; and they shall never perish, neither shall any man pluck them out of my hand. My father, which gave them me, is greater than all; and no man is able to pluck them out of my Fathers hand." Then John 6:37, says "All that the Father giveth me shall come to me; and him that cometh to me I will in no wise cast out." The born-again warrior has been adopted into the family and into the army of God on his salvation. John 1:12 says, "But as many as received him, to them gave he power to become the sons of God, even to them that believe on his name;" and Romans 8:15 says, "For ye have not received the spirit of bondage again to fear; but ye have received the Spirit of adoption, whereby we cry Abba, Father." And 1 Corinthians 3:16 says, "Know ye not that ye are the temple of God, and that the Spirit of God dwelleth in you?" It is the Spirit of God who protects the sinful Christian warrior from ever losing his salvation. Romans 5:8-9 says, "But God commendeth his love toward us, in that, while we were yet sinners, Christ died for us. Much more then, being now justified by his blood, we shall be saved from wrath through him."

Just as the soldier signs an oath of enlistment that is kept forever in the military archives, the Christian warrior's name is forever written in the Lamb's Book of life. The Apostle Paul tells his fellow Christian laborers that their names are written down in Philippians 4:3 when he says, "And I intreat thee also, true yokefellow, help those women which laboured with me in the gospel, with Clement also, and with other my fellow labourers, whose names are in the book of life." When the Christian's name is written down in the book of life it is forever; just as a person's birth certificate or adoption papers are forever and cannot be reversed. And to make the birth/adoption final Revelation 20 teaches about the final judgment and who shall enter into heaven. Verse 27 says, "And there shall in no wise enter into it any thing that defileth, neither whatsoever worketh abomination, or maketh a lie: but they which are written in the Lamb's book of life." To be born-again or adopted is forever, once saved always saved.

When a soldier is missing "in action" it is the result of enemy contact on the battlefield. A soldier may also be listed as "missing" in peacetime or not on deployment when he is unaccounted for and his whereabouts are unknown. In this instance the soldier may have been arrested by civilian law enforcement, or he may have been in a serious traffic accident and in a civilian hospital, or any other number of situations. In any event he will be listed at AWOL or absent without leave and after a thirty day period of "missing" he may be categorized as a deserter. A missing soldier is serious and every attempt to locate him is made by his unit and military officials. The position he holds in his unit is compromised and may cause his unit to become non-deployable and unable to accomplish its wartime mission.

It is also possible for the Christian warrior to become "missing in action" from his family unit and from his home church. It is always the result of sin in his life which has developed into a practice of "backsliding." The term "backsliding" used in Scripture always refers to the nation Israel turning its back on God. It refers to a Christian who has turned from their faith or a falling from a personal relationship with Jesus Christ into sin. Jeremiah 3:8 says, "And I saw, when for all the causes whereby backsliding Israel committed adultery I had put her away, and given her a bill of divorce; yet her treacherous sister Judah feared not, but went and played the harlot also." The warrior may have turned away from his Lord and Saviour, from his wife and family, from his employment, and from his church home.

When the Christian warrior is MIA from his home and family the consequences are frequently disastrous. The leadership is gone, the protection of wife and children is gone, the home is broken up and the walls of protection are gone. Everyone and everything in the family and home becomes a soft target for Satan and his devils. The family goes into a survival mode and can no longer focus on the mission. It is unlike the military warrior who goes MIA because soldiers are trained to take leadership immediately under combat conditions. The family unit is not trained for this and is dependent on the husband and father for leadership and guardianship. This is why Satan on the spiritual battlefield, just as the enemy on the unconventional battlefield, targets leadership.

When the Christian warrior is MIA from his home church an important part of the church family and unit is missing. Whatever ministry he was serving in is now affected. In the Book of Ephesians chapter four Paul describes the unity of the Saints with the Spirit and the church when he says in verse 16, "From whom the whole body fitly joined together and compacted by that which every joint supplieth, according to the effectual working in the measure of every part, maketh increase of the body unto the edifying of itself in love." Christ through the church joins believers together and unites them by the various ministries of the church which results in church growth and spiritual growth to its members. When a church member becomes MIA the church is missing a "fitted" and vital important part.

Just like the military service, no one in the church family is indispensable. The church and its ministries will continue and grow, but the MIA warrior will not receive the blessing of serving. Plus the testimony of the church family within the community it serves will be damaged.

There are two ways in which the Christian warrior may become KIA. The first is when he is killed while actively serving in a ministry at the time of his death. An example is the stoning of Stephen in Acts 8:59-60, "And they stoned Stephen, calling upon God, and saying, Lord Jesus, receive my spirit. And he kneeled down, and cried with a loud voice, Lord, lay not this sin to their charge. And when he had said this, he fell asleep." Scripture always refers to the death of a Christian as falling "asleep" or "giving up the ghost." Another example of this type of KIA is when a Christian dies while not actively serving in a ministry but is or has been active in the past.

A Christian warrior who dies may have been a lay person in the church, a pastor or deacon, Sunday school teacher or nursery worker. After accepting Jesus Christ by faith as his Lord and Saviour he may have never joined a Bible believing church, but after death he is assured that heaven is his home. An example would be Lazarus in Luke chapter sixteen. He is described as a man with sores who begged for crumbs to eat. Verse 21 says, "And desiring to be fed with the crumbs which fell from the rich man's table: moreover the dogs came and licked his sores." The chapter goes on to report that both the rich man and Lazarus died. The rich man lifted up his eyes in hell being in torment and begged for a drink of water from Lazarus who was being comforted in heaven while in the arms of Abraham. Another example would be Abraham who died of old age in Genesis 25:8, "Then Abraham gave up the ghost, and died in a good old age, an old man, and full of years; and was gathered to his people."

The second type of KIA is when the believer dies while backslidden and living a sinful life style. The believer may have returned to his old friends and his old sinful habits, or turned to new friends and new sinful habits for the physical pleasure of sin for a season. This type of Christian may continue his attendance in church, or he may ridicule those who attend church or those who profess salvation. He loses his salvation testimony and yields to the lust of the flesh, the lust of the eyes, and the pride of life. Galatians 5:19-21 give a list of the works of the flesh which are: adultery, fornication, uncleanness, lasciviousness, idolatry, witchcraft, hatred, variance, emulations, wrath, strife, seditions, heresies, envying, murders, drunkenness, and revellings. Those Christians who fall away into a backslidden state are tempting God. Galatians 6:7 says, "Be not deceived; God is not mocked: for whatsoever a man soweth, that shall he also reap." God will not allow a born-again Christian the privilege of salvation while at the same time mocking the commands of Scripture by his sinful life style. Matthew 6:24 says, "No man can serve two masters: for either he will hate the one, and love the other; or else he will hold to the one, and despise the other. Ye cannot serve God and mammon." The word "mammon" refers to the riches or pleasures of man.

The Christian warrior is commanded to live a separated life. 2 Timothy 2:4 says, "No man that warreth entangleth himself with the affairs of this life; that he may please him who hath chosen him to be a soldier." Just as a soldier in the military service today can be punished or discharged for his involvement in politics or disobeying lawful orders, etc., the Christian warrior may also suffer punishment. It is possible for God to cut short the physical life span of a believer and take him home early if he is mocking God by his disloyalty to His commands. God has and will "repent" or turn from His plans for a nation or an individual. Deuteronomy 32:36 says, "For the Lord shall judge his people, and repent himself for his servants, when he seeth that their power is gone, and there is none shut up, or left." God will not be mocked.

A Biblical example of a backslidden nation can be found in the book of Numbers chapter 14. The nation Israel has been freed from Egypt and Pharaoh and are about to enter into the Promised Land. Moses sends three spies into the land and after hearing their report the people are frightened and weep and murmur against Moses. God is angry and in verses 11-12 He says, "And the Lord said unto Moses, How long will this people provoke me? And how long will it be ere they believe me, for all the signs which I have shewed among them? I will smite them with the pestilence, and disinherit them…" Moses mediates to God for the people and God says in verse, 20 "…I have pardoned according to thy word." Then in verse 23 He says, "Surely they shall not see the land which I sware unto their fathers, neither shall any of them that provoked me see it." Then the death sentence is in verse 29, "Your carcasses shall fall in this wilderness; and all that were numbered of you. According to your whole number, from twenty years old and upward, which have murmured against me." So the nation Israel wandered in the wilderness for forty years until all the twenty year old men had died. They died, but went to heaven-God will not be mocked.

There was also a married couple named Ananias and Sapphira who are found in Acts chapter five. The prior chapter explains how the church members shared all they had with one another. Then in chapter five this married couple sold land and verse 2 says they, "…kept back part of the price, his wife also being privy to it, and brought a certain part, and laid it at the apostles' feet." In verse three and four the apostle Peter says to Ananias, "…why hath Satan filled thine heart to lie to the Holy Ghost, and to keep back part of the price of the land?…why hast thou conceived this thing in thine heart? Thou hast not lied unto men, but unto God." Verse 5 then gives the death sentence, "And Ananias hearing these words fell down, and gave up the ghost: and great fear came on all them that heard these things." A short time after this his wife

Sapphira comes to Peter (not knowing about her husband) and he asks her how much the land was sold for and she lies also . Verses 9-10 give her the death sentence saying, "...Peter said unto her, How is it that ye have agreed together to tempt the Spirit of the Lord? ...Then fell she down straightway at his feet, and yielded up the ghost..." They both died but went to heaven-God will not be mocked.

What the born-again warrior is doing at the time of his death does not affect his salvation. Remember, "once saved always saved." If he was wounded in action or missing in action prior to his death he is still saved and going to heaven, but God will not be mocked.

Victory on the Battlefield

"But thanks be to God, which giveth us the victory through our Lord Jesus Christ."

— 1 Corinthians 15:57

Since the Spiritual War has already been won on the cross of Calvary it is possible for the Christian warrior to win the daily battle. Remember I Timothy 1:18 says, "This charge I commit unto thee, son Timothy, according to the prophecies which went before on thee, that thou by them mightest war a good warfare." When the "war is good" you're winning. To survive and win on the spiritual battlefield requires leaders who have a personal relationship with Jesus Christ, who are trained for the spiritual battle, who pray continually, who read the Word of God daily, who are faithful, who fear the Lord, and who are strong and of good courage.

Every soldier knows his Commander- in- Chief and knows that he lives in the White House, Washington D.C. But does the Commander and Chief know the individual soldier-does he know his name and where he lives? The Christian Warrior has a personal relationship with his Commander-in-Chief and spends time with him every day. They know each other's thoughts, desires, fears, and dreams, they are in constant communication one with the other and never lose touch.

In order for the Christian warrior to be victorious on the Spiritual battlefield he must be faithful, able, able to teach, endure hardness in training and on the battlefield, and stay focused on the daily battle. 2 Timothy 2:2-4 says, "And the things that thou hast heard of me among many witnesses, the same commit thou to faithful men, who shall be able to teach others also. Thou therefore endure hardness, as a good soldier of Jesus Christ. No man that warreth entangleth himself with the affairs of this life; that he may please him who hath chosen him to be a soldier." He must also be fearless, strong and of good courage. These words are reminders in several verses of the Old Testament and Joshua 10:25, says "And Joshua said unto them, Fear not, nor be dismayed, be strong and of good courage: for thus shall the Lord do to all your enemies against whom ye fight."

Just as the combat soldier is faithful to his commander in accomplishing every mission and to those he leads in combat, the Christian warrior must be faithful to his commander-in-chief and to his family. The combat leader always puts the mission first and his men always, the Christian warrior must do likewise. The men of a team and family members must be confident of the faithfulness their leader has toward them and they will remain faithful and loyal to their leader and accomplish every mission.

The combat leader must be able to lead, be tactically and technically proficient in every weapon his team employs, able to teach and mentor new soldiers in tactics and weapons, survival, and to accomplish the mission. Likewise, the Christian warrior must be an able leader in the home, on the spiritual battlefield, and able to teach and mentor every family member in Satan's tactics for their survival and mission accomplishment.

The combat leader must be able to endure hardness. This is more than just physical strength and stamina; it includes the hardship of leadership on the battlefield. The combat leader is required to plan while his team is playing, to stay awake while his team is sleeping, to conduct a leader's recon while his team is resting, to acquire and redistribute ammunition and supplies while his team is under enemy fire, and to make decisions that may lead to death. To endure hardness also means to never accept defeat and to never give up, on yourself, your men, or the mission. The combat leader accepts full responsibilities for all his team accomplishes and fails to accomplish. The Christian warrior must develop this same type of personal dedication and hardness so his family can survive on the spiritual battlefield. He must have the physical strength and stamina to go to work all day, then come home to lead his family through the danger areas of public school, television, the internet and avoiding all the IED's set so maliciously by Satan.

An extreme example of the "hardness" of a combat soldier is the Medal of Honor citation of Master Sergeant Roy P. Benavidez, of Detachment B-56, 5th Special Forces Group, in the Republic of Vietnam. The citation reads: "On the morning of 2 May 1968, a 12-man Special Forces Reconnaissance Team was inserted by helicopters in a dense jungle area west of Loc Ninh, Viet Nam to gather intelligence information about confirmed large-scale enemy activity. This area was controlled and routinely patrolled by the North Vietnamese Army. After a short period of time on the ground, the team met heavy enemy resistance, and requested emergency extraction. Three helicopters attempted extraction, but were unable to land due to intense enemy small arms and anti-aircraft fire.

"Sergeant Benavidez was at the Forward Operating Base in Loc Ninh monitoring the operation by radio when these helicopters returned to off-load wounded crew members and to assess aircraft damage. Sergeant Benavidez voluntarily boarded a returning aircraft to assist in another extraction attempt. Realizing that all the team members were either dead or wounded and unable to move to the pickup zone, he directed the aircraft to a nearby clearing where he jumped from the hovering helicopter, and ran approximately 75 meters under withering small arms fire to the crippled team. Prior to reaching the team's position he was wounded in his right leg, face, and head. Despite these painful injuries, he took charge, repositioning the team members and directing their fire to facilitate the landing of an extraction aircraft, and the loading of wounded and dead team members. He then threw smoke canisters to direct the aircraft to the team's position.

"Despite his severe wounds and under intense enemy fire, he carried and dragged half of the wounded team members to the awaiting aircraft. He then provided protective fire by running alongside the aircraft as it moved to pick up the remaining team members. As the enemy's fire intensified, he hurried to recover the body and classified documents on the dead team leader. When he reached the leader's body, Sergeant Benavidez was severely wounded by small arms fire in the abdomen and grenade fragments in his back. At nearly the same moment, the aircraft pilot was mortally wounded, and his helicopter crashed.

"Although in extremely critical condition due to his multiple wounds, Sergeant Benavidez secured the classified documents and made his way back to the wreckage, where he aided the wounded out of the overturned aircraft, and gathered the stunned survivors into a defense perimeter. Under increasing enemy automatic weapons and grenade fire, he moved around the perimeter distributing water and ammunition to his weary men, reinstilling in them a will to live and fight. Facing a buildup of enemy opposition with a beleaguered team, Sergeant Benavidez mustered his strength, began calling in tactical air strikes and directed the fire from supporting gun ships to suppress the enemy's fire and so permit another extraction attempt. He was wounded again in his thigh by small arms fire while administering first aid to a wounded team member just before another extraction helicopter was able to land. His indomitable spirit kept him going as he began to ferry his comrades to the aircraft.

"On his second trip with the wounded, he was clubbed from behind and received additional wounds to his head and arms before killing his adversary. He then continued under devastating fire to carry the wounded to the helicopter. Upon reaching the aircraft, he spotted and killed two enemy soldiers who were rushing the craft from an angle that prevented the aircraft door gunner from firing upon them. With little strength remaining, he made one last trip to the perimeter to ensure that all classified material had been collected or destroyed, and to bring in the remaining wounded. Only then, in extremely serious condition from numerous wounds and loss of blood, did he allow himself to be pulled into the extraction aircraft.

"Sergeant Benavidez' gallant choice to join voluntarily his comrades who were in critical straits, to expose himself constantly to withering enemy fire, and his refusal to be stopped despite 57 wounds, saved the lives of at least eight men. His fearless personal leadership, tenacious devotion to duty, and extremely valorous actions in the face of overwhelming odds were in keeping with the highest traditions of the military service, and reflect the utmost credit on him and the United States Army." When asked why he did this he stated, "I just did what I was trained to do. Any Special Forces soldier would have done the same thing."

Master Sergeant Benavidez was a U.S. Army Special Forces soldier. He was faithful to his commander and the men in his command by coming to their aid, providing needed combat leadership on the unconventional battlefield, and enduring 57 wounds in rescuing a 12-man Special Forces "A" team. The Christian warrior on the spiritual battlefield must have the same tactical and technical skills, the same determination, the same endurance, the will to never quit and the combat leadership skills to be able to provide the purpose, direction, and motivation to accomplish the mission of his family while under the constant "wiles" of Satan.

How did Master Sergeant Benavidez become a mighty man of valor, by his personal desire and dedication to endure the hardness of training. The phrase "mighty man of valor" is used in the Bible several times and in each instance it describes men who have been victorious in battle. In the book of Judges the phrase is used by an angel of the LORD who is speaking to Gideon even before he has been tested in battle. In chapter six the angel finds Gideon threshing wheat behind a winepress because of his fear of the Midianites. Chapter 6 verse 12 states, "And the angel of the LORD appeared unto him (Gideon), and said unto him, The LORD is with thee, thou mighty man of valor." Only God knows if Master Sergeant Benavidez was a born-again Believer who had a personal relationship with Jesus Christ. If not, then he was a mighty man of valor because of his training. But, as Gideon, the Lord knows the heart of the Christian warrior. Yes he needs the training and experience to become a mighty man of valor and he receives it by trials, testing, and tribulations of the Lord. Romans 5:3-5 says, "And not only so, but we glory in tribulations also; knowing that tribulation worketh patience; and patience, experience; and experience, hope: And hope maketh not ashamed; because the love of God is shed abroad in our hearts by the Holy Ghost which is given unto us." Every trial, test and tribulation of the Christian warrior is for a purpose. Nothing is by luck, chance, fluke, mistake or circumstance, but by the providence of God.

Master Sergeant Benavidez did not entangle himself with politics, public opinion, trends, or current events. He kept his focus on being a combat soldier, his training, his preparation, and his mission on the battlefield. Prior to his one year combat deployment to Viet Nam he trained physically and mentally for every possible mission. When a soldier volunteers for Special Forces he knows that he will be tested in every area of soldiering, from Airborne training to specialized MOS training, from language school to survival school, from conventional warfare training to unconventional guerilla warfare training, from mountain warfare to jungle warfare and everything in-between. The

U.S. Army Special Forces qualification course takes from one and one half to two and one half years to complete depending on the Special Forces specialty. The training is long, hard, physically and mentally challenging. During his training he had no time to get himself entangled with the affairs of this life, only to focus on his training so he could accomplish any mission given by his Commander.

The Christian warrior must not entangle himself with the outside world either. Yes, he must remain knowledgeable of world events and know who to vote for etc., but he must not get entangled to the point that they take priority over his family and his relationship with Jesus Christ. He must remain focused on leading his family team throughout the spiritual battlefield.

There is no doubt that Master Sergeant Benavidez was fearless, strong and of good courage. Let us examine how an ordinary man becomes fearless, strong and of good courage. The word "fearless" is defined as a person who is free from fear of great bodily harm or death, or fearless of consequences; someone who is bold and courageous. The word "strong" is more than having great physical strength but also having an ability to bear or endure; having a strong constitution; a man of strong judgment or imagination. And the word "courage" refers to a man who is able to encounter danger and difficulties with firmness, or without fear or depression of spirits; to possess valor and boldness; courage which arises from a sense of duty.

These are the identical words used by God throughout the Bible when He is encouraging His mighty men of valor to go to war. These words were directed to the nation Israel as they first entered the promised land in Deuteronomy 31:6-7, "Be strong and of a good courage, fear not…" He said these same words to Joshua in 1:9, "Have not I commanded thee? Be strong and of a good courage; be not afraid…" and 1:18, "…only be strong and of a good courage." Israel, led by Joshua went on to conquer the walled city of Jericho, then the Armies of the

Amorites, the Perizzites, the Canaanites, the Hittites, the Girgashites, the Hivites, and the Jebusites.

Master Sergeant Benavidez acquired these traits by his own determination, fortitude, training and experience. All of his Special Forces training was by the book and he was a soldier who went by the book. He learned to talk the talk of a soldier and he learned to walk the walk of a soldier. Many times military training is monotonous because it is repetitive. But the repetition has a purpose; when a soldier is confronted with a life or death decision or experience, without thinking he automatically does what he has been trained to do. His training takes over because he has been confronted with identical circumstances in training. He knows what to do, how to do it, and how to lead his men. It has been said "sweat on the training field saves blood on the battlefield." When a soldier responds to a dangerous situation, his training instincts take over, his mind and body react as they have been trained too, and his muscle memory takes over. When the situation has passed, other soldiers say he was "fearless", but in reality he was reacting to his training instinct for survival. Yes, soldiers are in fear of dangerous situations but they do not let the fear stop them from performing their duty they have trained to do.

Every battlefield is dangerous. Master Sergeant Benavidez had fear as he climbed into that helicopter to assist the "A" Team, but his training took over. He did not have to think about what to do he reacted to the situation and did what was necessary as each situation developed and presented itself. He was not a member of that particular Special Forces "A" Team. It did not matter that he was a junior Non-Commissioned Officer (Staff Sergeant) at the time (Each "A" Team is commanded by a Captain with a Warrant Officer as XO, a Master Sergeant as Team Sergeant, and each team has three or four Sergeant's First Class with junior NCO's completing the team), they needed immediate assistance and he was available.

Every combat team on today's lethal battlefield has tremendous fire-power available to him. The team leader can call for QRF (quick reaction forces) reinforcements, artillery, helicopter or AC130H Spectre gunships, fast movers (A-10's and up) to smart bombs and cruise missiles. Master Sergeant Benavidez called for the air assets that were available to him in Viet Nam, enabling him to save the team.

The Christian warrior on the spiritual battlefield has reinforcements that are incalculable. Deuteronomy 31:6 says, "Be strong and of a good courage, fear not, nor be afraid of them: for the Lord thy God, he it is that doth go with thee; he will not fail thee, nor forsake thee." God always tells his servants to be not afraid and of good courage because: Deuteronomy 31:23, "…and I will be with thee," Joshua 1:9, "…for the Lord thy God is with thee whithersoever thou goest," 1 Chronicles 28:20 "…be strong and of good courage, and do it: fear not, nor be dismayed: for the Lord God, even my God, will be with thee; he will not fail thee, nor forsake thee, until thou has finished all the work for the service of the house of the Lord," Hebrews 13:5, "..for he hath said, I will never leave thee, nor forsake thee," and Matthew 28:10 says, "…I am with you always, even unto the end of the world…"

The Christian warrior can call on the Lord at any time and on any battlefield and he will be there.

The spiritual army of God is always at the prayerful call of the Christian warrior on the spiritual battlefield. Just as the commander on today's battlefield supplies all that is required for mission accomplishment the Lord supplies all that is required for the Christian warrior on the spiritual battlefield.

Sergeant Major Stan Parker was an infantryman in the 101st Airborne Division, Viet Nam in 1968-69. His company was on a search and destroy mission and were ambushed by the North Vietnamese Army (NVA). He was wounded in the leg and other wounded members of his squad required immediate medical evacuation. They were all moved to a pick-up zone and placed into a medivac helicopter. The NVA observed the pick-up zone and as the helicopter lifted off with the wounded they initiated heavy machine gun fire and RPG rounds (rocket propelled grenades). As Sergeant Parker lay inside the helicopter he heard the RPG and machine gun fire increase and saw the machine gun tracer rounds go in and out through the skin of the aircraft and saw the helicopter insulation floating inside the aircraft. When the RPG round hit the aircraft it exploded and crashed.

When Sergeant Parker regained consciousness he was lying in tall grass approximately 30 feet away from the burning aircraft. He was lying on his M-16, his leg was still bleeding and broken, and he could see and hear NVA soldiers walking through the high grass and across the open pick-up zone. Suddenly, he heard the sound of M-16 and M-60 machine gun fire (distinctive U.S. weapon fire) and saw the NVA run off the pick-up zone. After a few minutes he saw and heard 101st soldiers around the downed medivac helicopter that he was thrown out of, searching for and helping the casualties who were on the aircraft and the injured and wounded crew members. Sergeant Parker attempted to yell out to them but he lost his voice. He attempted to get onto his feet or to crawl toward them through the tall grass but was too weak. He tried to lift up his arms to wave but couldn't. He could only watch as the soldiers quickly gathered the wounded and watched as another medivac helicopter landed in the same pick-up zone. He made one final physical effort to be noticed but was unable. As the medivac began to lift off and the U.S. soldiers began taking defensive positions to safeguard the helicopter the NVA again began AK-47 and machine gun fire at the aircraft.

Just as Sergeant Parker was about to give up, a U.S. soldier came from behind and helped him to his feet. The soldier stood at his left placing his right hand around Sergeant Parker's waist and holding Sergeant Parker's left hand which was around the soldiers neck. Sergeant Parker was holding his M-16 across his chest with his right hand as they both hobbled to the aircraft which was at a low hover. They were walking toward the left front of the aircraft and Sergeant Parker made eye contact with the left seat pilot. The aircraft immediately stopped its assent and the aircraft door gunner made eye contact with Sergeant Parker and waived for him to hurry. As they neared the hovering aircraft two NVA soldiers came running out of the tree line firing their weapons attempting to shoot it down. Due to their avenue of approach only Sergeant Parker and the left seat pilot could see their approach. As Sergeant Parker and the soldier carrying him hobbled quickly toward the awaiting aircraft Sergeant Parker was able to fire his weapon and kill both NVA soldiers. As he did so the left seat pilot gave him a "thumbs up." Finally Sergeant Parker was placed into the medivac aircraft and as it lifted off he was praying it would not get shot down.

It was about a twenty minute flight to the 101st Airborne Division compound where they landed. As Sergeant Parker was lifted off the aircraft he turned toward the door gunner and asked for the soldier who helped him into the aircraft to thank him for saving his life. The door gunner said that he didn't see anyone helping him into the aircraft. He said, yeah, I mean the "troop" who picked me up from the crash site and carried me to your chopper. The door gunner said he didn't know who he was talking about. Sergeant Parker then asked to talk to the left seat pilot because he knew that he saw the soldier carrying him from the tall grass, kill the two NVA soldiers and hobble to the aircraft. The pilot said he did not see anyone with Sergeant Parker and did not see anyone pick him up or carry him. He related to Sergeant Parker that he saw him pick himself up from the tall grass, hobble funny toward the aircraft by himself, kill the two NVA soldiers then climb into the aircraft by himself. Sergeant Parker then asked the rest of the men who were still in the aircraft where the soldier was who helped him. Every man said that Sergeant Parker was by himself and that no one helped him from the time he picked himself up from the tall grass until he was inside the aircraft.

VICTORY ON THE BATTLEFIELD

Sergeant Parker (now Sergeant Major) was a born-again believer, saved and protected by Jesus Christ. Who was the soldier that picked him up wounded from the battlefield and carried him to the waiting medivac helicopter? It was his Lord and Saviour who promised to never leave him nor forsake him. The same "angel" who called out Abraham from the city of Ur; the same angel who brought the horses and chariots of fire that protected the prophet Elisha and his servant; the same angel who followed and saved the nation Israel from the Egyptian army; the same angel who destroyed the Egyptian army in the Red Sea; the same angel who ministered to Elijah with food and drink; the same angel who shut the lions mouths against Daniel; the same angel who protects the saints from harm in Exodus 32:2, "And I will send an angel before thee; and I will drive out the Canaanite, the Amorite, and the Hittite, and the Perizzite, the Hivite, and the Jubusite."

The same angel will look out for you today if you are a child of God. Many military service members who are deployed to Iraq and Afghanistan today carry with them the 91st Psalm and many have the Psalm memorized. (See enclosure #4.) This psalm gives reassurance to the Christian warrior of God's protection on and off the spiritual battlefield. Matthew 28:10 says, "…I am with you always, even unto the end of the world. Amen…"; Hebrew 13:5 says, "…I will never leave thee, nor forsake thee"; John 14:8 says, "I will not leave you comfortless: I will come to you."

Just as a father knows where his children are, just as the First Sergeant knows where his soldiers are, our heavenly Father knows where all of His children are located. On today's lethal battlefield soldiers are sometimes required to carry a GPS so his exact location can be monitored. If the soldier (or team) comes under enemy fire a Quick Reaction Force can be immediately dispatched to his known location. If the soldier requests artillery or air support his exact location must be known so he is not a victim of friendly fire. Or if he request's a helicopter for immediate extraction or medivac his location is already known.

The military's GPS system is excellent and has probably saved hundreds of lives. The soldier is only required to keep the "tool" maintained, extra batteries, and he must be in a position that offers no hindrance to satellite communication. The more satellites he can communicate with offers a more exact location.

The Christian warrior on the spiritual battlefield is also monitored. When he received Jesus Christ as his Lord and Saviour he received the Lord's GPS. At the moment of salvation the Christian warrior received the Holy Spirit who now takes up residence in his body. The Holy Spirit is God's "seal" of ownership. 1 Corinthians 3:16 says, "Know ye not that ye are the temple of God, and that the Spirit of God dwelleth in you?" 2 Timothy 2:19 says, "Nevertheless the foundation of God standeth sure, having this seal, The Lord knoweth them that are his..." And Ephesians 4:30 confirms this by saying, "And grieve not the holy Spirit of God, whereby ye are sealed unto the day of redemption."

Every born again believer has God's "seal." Just as the military can track every soldier on the battlefield by satellite and GPS, God tracks each of His children by the seal of the Holy Spirit. God's system of tracking never needs batteries and is never hindered. When the Lord's warrior needs assistance or support of any kind he does not need radio communication. He only needs to pray. At times he does not even have to request assistance because God knows all his needs and supplies them before he even asks. Matthew 6:8 says, "Be not ye therefore like unto them: for your Father knoweth what things ye have need of, before ye ask him." And Philippians' 4:19, says "But my God shall supply all your need according to his riches in glory by Christ Jesus."

When a Christian warrior prays for assistance and protection God always answers. At times the answered prayer comes just as we requested; the arrival of the quick reaction force, a gun ship, a medivac helicopter, or additional ammunition. Sometimes God answers our prayer but not in a way we understand. During World War II, a U.S. Marine was separated from his unit on a Pacific island. The fighting had been intense, and in the smoke and crossfire he had lost touch with his comrades. Alone in the jungle, he could hear enemy soldiers coming in his direction. Scrambling for cover, he found his way up a high ridge to several small caves in the rock. Quickly, he crawled inside one of the caves. Although safe for the moment, he realized that once the enemy soldiers looking for him swept up the ridge, they would quickly search all the caves and he would be killed.

As he waited, he prayed, "Lord, if it be your will, please protect me. Whatever you will though, I love you and trust you. Amen." After praying, he lay quietly listening to the enemy begin to draw close. He thought, "Well, I guess the Lord isn't going to help me out of this one." Then he saw a spider begin to build a web over the front of his cave. As he watched, listening to the enemy searching for him all the while, the spider layered strand after strand of web across the opening of the cave. "Ha" he thought, "What I need is a brick wall and what the Lord has sent me is a spider web. God does have a sense of humor."

As the enemy drew closer he watched from the darkness of his hideout and could see them searching one cave after another. As they came to his, he got ready to make his last stand. To his amazement, however, after glancing in the direction of his cave, they moved on. Suddenly, he realized that with the spider web over the entrance, his cave looked as if no one had entered for quite a while. "Lord, forgive me," prayed the young Marine. "I had forgotten that in you a spider's web is stronger than a brick wall."

Christian soldiers today must also obey commands they sometimes don't understand. But every soldier knows he must obey those in lawful authority over them. Soldiers on the modern lethal battlefield must have faith and trust in their commander so they can accomplish their mission. The Christian soldier must also have the same faith and trust in their commander so they can accomplish their mission and gain victory on the spiritual battlefield. God Bless America and every soldier on the battlefield.

Coming Home/War's End

"And God shall wipe away all tears from their eyes; and there shall be no more death, neither sorrow, nor crying, neither shall there be any more pain: for the former things are passed away."

– Revelation 21:4

Going home is what every serviceman looks forward to while deployed in a combat zone. He is going home to a spouse, family and friends. Some refer to going home as going "back to the real world" because the battlefield is so unreal. The noise of battle, the fog of war, the roar of aircraft, the sounds of an M3 carbine, an AK-47, an RPG, artillery fire, the dreadful fearful sound of incoming rockets, the cry of the wounded, and the cry for the dead. It all ends when you're home, except for those terrible dreams that still haunt you. ("Doc" Bradley the Navy Corpsman who was one of the flag raisers in the famous Iwo Jima photo of WW2, cried in his sleep for four years after the war.)

The time in a combat zone varies for each military service. Generally, a Sailor and Airman are deployed to Afghanistan for four months, a Marine for 7 months, and an Army soldier for 12 months. There are exceptions for each military branch depending on the specialty of the service member and their unit of assignment. But "going home" is just as important for the military inspector or civilian Department of Defense official who visits for a few days or a few weeks.

Just as the military aircraft brought the soldier into the combat zone from a high, quick and steep descent onto the airfield to avoid enemy rockets the aircraft departs in the same manner. Hours later the pilot makes an announcement to all passengers that the aircraft has left enemy airspace. A loud, thunderous shout of enthusiasm mixed with relief and tears of joy come from every soldier. Every soldier is saying to himself "I made it, I'm going home."

Going home means rest, relaxation, and sleep. There is no more dread of what may occur to you when you leave a safe area. You can put your guard down, there is no need to carry your weapon and combat load everywhere you go. There is no more fear of IED's in the roadway or incoming rockets, you're home.

At home is where those warriors who were killed-in-action are memorialized. There is neither time nor a safe location in a combat zone to have a proper service. No time for friends or superiors to recognize the warrior's dedication and faithful service in a time of war to his fellow soldiers, his unit, and his country. Home is the warrior's final resting place.

At home is also where the warrior is recognized for his personal valor and achievement during his deployment in a combat zone. Military formations are conducted and service members are called forward to be rewarded for their actions. Some receive medals and some receive commendations for their service. But they are all just glad to be home.

The Christian warrior on the spiritual battlefield will also get called home. The warrior on the battlefield is deployed for a specific period of service from four months to twelve months. Many warriors today serve multiple tours of duty in Iraq and Afghanistan. But the Christian warrior never leaves the spiritual battlefield. He is in a life-long battle; he is in spiritual warfare for the duration of the war - until he is called to his heavenly home.

In the early 1920's an elderly man and his wife were returning home after serving many years as missionaries. As the ocean liner neared the dock all the passengers lined the rails looking for relatives and friends who would welcome them home. As they looked down from the rails of the ship there were hundreds of people, there was a band, there were U.S. flags and streamers of "Welcome Home" and there was a temporary stage set up with city officials in attendance. The elderly missionary couple looked down and saw standing at the front row of the large crowd the pastor and his wife who had been supporting him prayerfully and financially all these years. The missionary looked over to his wife and said, "What a welcome home."

The missionary couple took their position in the long line to disembark the ocean liner and walk down the gangplank onto U.S. soil again. As they neared the gangplank a couple who were ahead of them were introduced from the temporary stage set up on the dock. They were famous film stars. The band starting playing, the crowd shouted out welcome home, streamers were thrown, the film stars were mobbed from all their fans, the city officials gave them the "key" to the city and they were driven off with the crowd following them. As the missionary couple took their turn to walk down the gangplank the band had already stopped playing, the large welcoming crowd was almost entirely gone, the streamers were lying on the dock, the temporary stage was being dismantled, and there were only a few people left on the dock, which included the faithful pastor and his wife. The pastor could see the look of disappointment on the missionary couple's face who thought the welcome home was for their years of faithful service and he said, "You're not home yet."

As you recall, the Christian warrior is referred to as a stranger, sojourner, ambassador, and pilgrim throughout Scripture. This is because his home has not been on earth since he accepted Jesus Christ as his Lord and Saviour and joined the Army and family of God. Romans 8:15 says, "...ye have received the Spirit of adoption, whereby we cry, Abba, Father." And Galatians 3:26 says, "For ye are all the children of God by faith in Christ Jesus." Just as the soldier on the battlefield today is hunted, persecuted, shot and killed, the Christian warrior is also persecuted on the Spiritual battlefield. The Christian is warned several times in Scripture of persecution and is told to be glad for it in Matthew 5:11-12 which says, "Blessed are ye, when men shall revile you, and persecute you, and shall say all manner of evil against you falsely, for my sake. Rejoice, and be exceeding glad: for great is your reward in heaven: for so persecuted they the prophets which were before you."

If you have been born-again you will be persecuted in one way or another. When Paul was an unsaved Jewish Pharisee, he was praised and honored, but after he accepted Jesus Christ as his Lord and Saviour he was persecuted and hated. Jesus said of Paul in Acts 9:16, "For I will shew him how great things he must suffer for my name's sake." Then in 2 Corinthians the suffering of Paul is outlined in 11:22-33(1) as he related receiving 39 stripes (whippings) five times from the Jews, three times beaten with rods, stoned once, in three shipwrecks, robbed and beaten, in perils by the heathen-in the city-in the wilderness-and in the sea, he hungered and thirsted, and was left cold and naked. All Christians will suffer while living physically on this earth, but will be rewarded when they go home to glory.

Just as Jesus and His angels rejoice when a sinner is saved, they rejoice also at his coming home. Luke 15:10, says "Likewise, I say unto you, there is joy in the presence of the angels of God over one sinner that repenteth." When a sinner gets saved he is sanctified and indwelt by the Holy Spirit. At physical death the soul of the saved sinner goes directly to heaven and is in the immediate presence of the Lord. 2 Corinthians

5:8 says, "We are confident, I say, and willing rather to be absent from the body, and to be present with the Lord." God as our heavenly father looks forward and rejoices at our coming home. Psalm 116:15 says, "Precious in the sight of the Lord is the death of his saints." This truly is "coming home."

Just as the soldier receives his reward at home, the Christian warrior also receives his reward on his return to his heavenly home. In John 14:2 Jesus is saying, "In my Father's house are many mansions: if it were not so, I would have told you. I go to prepare a place for you." And just as the modern warrior on the battlefield the Spiritual warrior will receive a reward that is proportionate to his service. Revelation 22:12 says to the Christian warrior, "And, behold, I come quickly; and my reward is with me, to give every man according as his work shall be." And Matthew 6:4 says, "...and thy Father which seeth in secret himself shall reward thee openly." The Bible teaches there are five spiritual crowns to receive:

1. The Incorruptible Crown mentioned in 1 Corinthians 9:25, "And every man that striveth for the mastery is temperate in all things. Now they do it to obtain a corruptible crown; but we an incorruptible."

2. The Crown of Righteousness mentioned in 2 Timothy 4:8, "Henceforth there is laid up for me a crown of righteousness, which the Lord, the righteous judge, shall give me at that day: and not to me only, but unto all them also that love his appearing."

3. The Crown of Life mentioned in James 1:12, "Blessed is the man that endureth temptation: for when he is tried, he shall receive the crown of life, which the Lord hath promised to them that love him."

4. The Crown of Glory mentioned in 1 Peter 5:4, "And when the chief Shepherd shall appear, ye shall receive a crown of glory that fadeth not away."

5. The Crown of Rejoicing mentioned in 1 Thessalonians 2:19, "For what is our hope, or joy, or crown of rejoicing? Are not even ye in the presence of our Lord Jesus Christ at his coming?"

The Christian warrior will also receive his inheritance as an adopted child of God. As such he becomes a joint-heir with Jesus Christ which has been guaranteed by the "seal" of God. Remember that Romans 8:15 teaches that believers, "...have received the Spirit of adoption..." And Romans goes on to say in 8:17, "And if children, then heirs; heirs of God, and joint heirs with Christ; if so be that we suffer with him, that we may be also glorified together." 1 Peter 1:4 mentions the inheritance which we can only imagine, "To an inheritance incorruptible, and undefiled, and that fadeth not away, reserved in heaven for you." We will also receive a glorified body in heaven. Philippians 3:20-21 says, "For our conversation is in heaven; from whence also we look for the Saviour, the Lord Jesus Christ: Who shall change our vile body, that it may be fashioned like unto his glorious body..." The Christian warrior will also receive a new retirement home custom designed by Jesus Himself. He assures this in John 14:2 when he says, "In my Father's house are many mansions: if it were not so, I would have told you. I go to prepare a place for you." All of these unbelievable rewards are guaranteed by God the Holy Spirit in Ephesians 4:30 which says, "And grieve not the holy Spirit of God, whereby ye are sealed unto the day of redemption." The born-again Christian cannot even imagine the heavenly rewards awaiting his return home.

Instead of full retirement the Christian warrior will continue to serve his Lord and Saviour for all eternity, and enjoy every minute of it. As the soldier who enlists in the service, he begins a military career. After Basic Training and after specialty training he continues his service as long as he remains in the military. Many service members who leave the military continue in the same or a related field in the civilian community taking full advantage of the military training and experience they obtained. As you visit with military veterans you will find that the vast majority regret leaving the military after a short term of service and wishing they had remained until retirement. This never occurs to the Christian warrior in his service to his Lord and Saviour Jesus Christ. Upon being called and entering the family and army of God his service has been planned and set for all eternity. 2 Timothy 1:9 says, "Who hath saved us, and called us with a holy calling, not according to our works, but according to his own purpose and grace, which was given us in Christ Jesus before the world began." God has an eternal plan for every Christian warrior that goes beyond our physical presence on earth for seventy plus years.

The "plan" is to serve God whereever He has placed you. Every service member is obedient to his commander just as every Christian warrior is obedient to his Commander. The warrior today obeys all orders of his commander and does so wholeheartedly, courageously and enthusiastically, no matter where he is stationed or deployed. The Christian warrior should be just as obedient. Deuteronmy13:4 says, "Ye shall walk after the Lord your God, and fear him, and keep his commandments, and obey his voice, and ye shall serve him, and cleave unto him." No matter where you live, where you work, where you're deployed, and no matter what New Testament bible believing church you belong, there is a ministry for you. God placed you in that location and position for His glory. Following orders, obeying commands, being diligent in the performance of duties and responsibilities is what soldiers have been trained to do-more so for the Christian warrior while a "stranger" on earth. And after this brief seventy or eighty years of life on earth, God also has a plan for the born-again believer on the new heaven and earth.

Scripture teaches the Second Coming of Christ in Revelation chapter 19:11-16(2). These verses teach Christ riding down from heaven on a white horse and fulfilling prophecy of His twofold role of judge and warrior. Verse 14 says, "And the armies which were in heaven followed him upon white horses, clothed in fine linen, white and clean." The "armies" refer to all born-again Christians who physically died (gave up the ghost) who have been residing in heaven until this time. These Christian warriors have new uniforms of fine white clean linen, not the camouflage uniforms of today. 1 Thessalonians 4 refers to those born again Christians who are still physically alive at His coming in verse 17, "Then we which are alive and remain shall be caught up together with them in the clouds, to meet the Lord in the air: and so shall we ever be with the Lord." His army will destroy the army of Satan at the battle of Armageddon mentioned in Revelation chapter 20.

Immediately after this Revelation chapter 20:1-3(3) explains that an angel comes down from heaven who lays hold of Satan and binds him in a bottomless pit, set with a seal, for a thousand years. This is the beginning of the millennial reign and kingdom of Jesus Christ on earth. Verse three concludes the thousand years by saying, "...that he (Satan) should deceive the nations no more, till the thousand years should be fulfilled: and after that he must be loosed a little season." For one thousand years there will be no satanic influence on the earth after Jesus physically returns to rule and reign. This will result in untold blessings on earth such as: peace on earth, Isaiah 2:4(4), the perfect administration of justice, Isaiah 9:7(5), no sickness and the healing of the deformed, Isaiah 29:17-19(6) and 33:24(7), economic prosperity to all people and nations, Isaiah 30:23(8) and Joel 2:21-27(9), a unified worship and language, Isaiah 45:23(10) and Zephaniah 3:9(11).

During this one thousand year reign of Christ on earth every Christian warrior will have a duty and responsibility to perform. These duties will be rewarding and fulfilling for every soldier. It is the ideal duty that every soldier wished for. This is all part of His plan for every child of God who will live with Him for all eternity. Titus 1:2 says, "In hope of eternal life, which God, that cannot lie, promised before the world began."

The Millennial Reign of Christ ends in Revelation 20:7 which says, "And when the thousand years are expired, Satan shall be loosed out of his prison." Satan will then make another last attempt to defeat Christ by gathering another army from the unsaved people on earth who rejected Jesus Christ as Lord and Saviour. Verse 9 then says, "And they went up on the breadth of the earth, and compassed the camp of the saints about, and the beloved city (Jerusalem): and fire came down from God out of heaven, and devoured them." This Divine destruction of Satan, his angels and his army of rebels, witnessed by every Christian warrior will be their last combat military action. Then Revelation 7:10-15(12) describe the end of Satan, his fallen angels, the anti-Christ, the false prophet of the Tribulation period, and the lost. They are all cast into the lake of fire and verse 15 says, "And whosoever was not found written in the book of life was cast into the lake of fire." The lost unbelievers spend the rest of eternity suffering in the lake of fire.

The Christian warrior who has lived in this church age serving the Lord Jesus and then served during the Millennial Reign of Christ still has all eternity to serve Him. Jesus still has a plan for each believer in the new heaven and earth.

Chapters 21-22 of Revelation then tell of a new heaven and new earth which was predicted by Isaiah in 65:17 which says, "For, behold, I create new heavens and a new earth: and the former shall not be remembered, nor come into mind." God in his mercy will end the crying of the Christian warrior of all that he has suffered through physically on earth, of all that he witnessed during the millennial reign, and the destruction of the army of Satan. Chapter 21:4 says, "And God shall wipe away all tears from their eyes; and there shall be no more death neither sorrow, nor crying, neither shall there be any more pain: for the former things are passed away."

These chapters describe how the present universe will be cleansed from all the effects of sin. 2 Peter 3:7 says, "But the heavens and the earth, which are now, by the same word are kept in store, reserved unto fire against the day of judgment and perdition of ungodly men." God will forever live with His redeemed people and there will be no tears, death, sorrow, crying, or pain. All of God's saints (every Christian warrior) will serve him and reign with Him for ever. Daniel 7:18 says, "But the saints of the most High shall take the kingdom, and possess the kingdom for ever, even for ever and ever." And verse 27 of the same chapter continues with "And the kingdom and dominion, and the greatness of the kingdom under the whole heaven, shall be given to the people of the saints of the most High, whose kingdom is an everlasting kingdom, and all dominions shall serve and obey him."

To spend all eternity with God in His heavenly kingdom is the Christian warrior's final duty station. Amen.

Scripture References

The Battlefield

1. Ephesians 2:2 Wherein in time past ye walked according to the course of this world, according to the prince of the power of the air, the spirit that now worketh in the children of disobedience:

2. Timothy 2:26 And that they may recover themselves out of the snare of the devil, who are taken captive by him at his will.

3. Corinthians 11:13 For such are false apostles, deceitful workers, transforming themselves into the apostles of Christ.

4. Luke 4:6 And the devil said unto him, All this power will I give thee, and the glory of them: for that is delivered unto me; and to whomsoever I will I give it.

5. Ten Commandments, Exodus chapter 20 verses 3-17.

    (1) Thou shalt have no other gods before me.

    (2) Thou shalt not make unto thee any graven image, or any

likeness of any thing that is in heaven above, or that is in the earth beneath, or that is in the water under the earth.

(3) Thou shalt not take the name of the LORD thy God in vain; for the LORD will not hold him guiltless that taketh his name in vain.

(4) Remember the sabbath day, to keep it holy.

(5) Honour thy father and thy mother: that thy days may be long upon the land which the LORD thy God giveth thee. (A command with a promise)

(6) Thou shalt not kill.

(7) Thou shalt not commit adultery.

(8) Thou shalt not steal.

(9) Thou shalt not bear false witness against thy neighbour.

(10) Thou shalt not covet thy neighbour's house, thou shalt not covet thy neighbour's wife, nor his manservant, nor his maidservant, nor his ox, nor his ass, nor any thing that is thy neighbour's.

6. Romans 8:15 For ye have not received the spirit of bondage again to fear; but ye have received the Spirit of adoption, whereby we cry, Abba, Father.

7. 1 Corinthians 16:13 Watch ye, stand fast in the faith, quit you like men, be strong.

8. 2 Timothy 2:1 Thou therefore, my son, be strong in the grace that is in Christ Jesus.

9. 1 Kings 2:2 I go the way of all the earth: be thou strong therefore, and shew thyself a man;

10. Isaiah 35:4 Say to them that are of a fearful heart, Be strong, fear not: behold, your God will come with vengeance, even God with a recompense; he will come and save you.

11. 2 Chronicles 15:7 Be ye strong therefore, and let not your hands be weak: for your work shall be rewarded.

12. Exodus 14:14 The LORD shall fight for you, and ye shall hold your peace.

13. Exodus 23:27 I will send my fear before thee, and will destroy all the people to whom thou shalt come, and I will make all thine enemies turn their backs unto thee

14. 2 Chronicles 20:29 And the fear of God was on all the kingdoms of those countries, when they had heard that the LORD fought against the enemies of Israel.

15. 2 Chronicles 32:8 With him is an arm of flesh; but with us is the LORD our God to help us, and to fight our battles. And the people rested themselves upon the words of Hezekiah king of Judah.

The Enemy

1. 2 Corinthians 4:4 In whom the god of this world hath blinded the minds of them which believe not, lest the light of the glorious gospel of Christ, who is the image of God, should shine unto them.

2. Revelation 12:9 And the great dragon was cast out, that old serpent, called the Devil, and Satan, which deceiveth the whole world: he was cast out into the earth, and his angels were cast out with him.

3. Mark 16:17 And these signs shall follow them that believe; In my name shall they cast out devils; they shall speak with new tongues;

4. Luke 10:17 And the seventy returned again with joy, saying, Lord, even the devils are subject unto us through thy name.

5. 1 Corinthians 10:21 Ye cannot drink the cup of the Lord, and the cup of devils: ye cannot be partakers of the Lord's table, and of the table of devils.

6. Mark 9:18 And wheresoever he taketh him, he teareth him: and he foameth, and gnasheth with his teeth, and pineth away: and I spake to thy disciples that they should cast him out; and they could not.

7. Matthew 12:22 Then was brought unto him one possessed with a devil, blind, and dumb: and he healed him, insomuch that the blind and dumb both spake and saw.

8. Luke 13:11 And, behold, there was a woman which had a spirit of infirmity eighteen years, and was bowed together, and could in no wise lift up herself.

9. Luke 8:26-36 And they arrived at the country of the Gadarenes, which is over against Galilee.

   And when he went forth to land, there met him out of the city a certain man, which had devils long time, and ware no clothes, neither abode in any house, but in the tombs. When he saw Jesus, he cried out, and fell down before him, and with a loud voice said, What have I to do with thee, Jesus, thou Son of God most high? I beseech thee, torment me not. (For he had commanded the unclean spirit to come out of the man. For oftentimes it had caught him: and he was kept bound with chains and in fetters; and he brake the bands, and was driven of the devil into the wilderness.) And Jesus asked him, saying, What is thy name? And he said, Legion: because many devils were entered into him. And they besought him that he would not command them to go out into the deep. And there was there an herd of many swine feeding on the mountain: and they besought him that he would suffer them to enter into them. And he suffered them. Then went the devils out of the man, and entered into the swine: and the herd ran violently down a steep place into the lake, and were choked. When they that fed them saw what was done, they fled, and went and told it in the city and in the country. Then they went out to see what was done; and came to Jesus, and found the man, out of whom the devils were departed, sitting at the feet of Jesus, clothed, and in his right mind: and they were afraid. They also which saw it told them by what means he that was possessed of the devils was healed.

10. Mark 9:22 And often times it hath cast him into the fire, and into the waters, to destroy him: but if thou anst do any thing, have compassion on us, and help us.

Leadership on the Battlefield and in the Home

1. Deuteronomy 25:5-10 If brethren dwell together, and one of them die, and have no child, the wife of the dead shall not marry without unto a stranger: her husband's brother shall go in unto her, and take her to him to wife, and perform the duty of an husband's brother unto her. And it shall be, that the firstborn which she beareth shall succeed in the name of his brother which is dead, that his name be not put out of Israel. And if the man like not to

take his brother's wife, then let his brother's wife go up to the gate unto the elders, and say, My husband's brother refuseth to raise up unto his brother a name in Israel, he will not perform the duty of my husband's brother. Then the elders of his city shall call him, and speak unto him: and if he stand to it, and say, I like not to take her; Then shall his brother's wife come unto him in the presence of the elders, and loose his shoe from off his foot, and spit in his face, and shall answer and say, So shall it be done unto that man that will not build up his brother's house. And his name shall be called in Israel, The house of him that hath his shoe loosed.

The Soldier's and Leader's Manual

1. Joshua 8:3 So Joshua arose, and all the people of war, to go up against Ai: and Joshua chose out thirty thousand mighty men of valour, and sent them away by night.

2. Joshua 10:7 So Joshua ascended from Gilgal, he, and all the people of war with him, and all the mighty men of valour.

3. 2 Kings 24:14 And he carried away all Jerusalem, and all the princes, and all the mighty men of valour, even ten thousand captives, and all the craftsmen and smiths: none remained, save the poorest sort of the people of the land.

4. 1 Chronicles 5:24 And these were the heads of the house of their fathers, even Epher, and Ishi, and Eliel, and Azriel, and Jeremiah, and Hodaviah, and Jahdiel, mighty men of valour, famous men, and heads of the house of their fathers.

Hard Target

1. Matthew 25:35 For I was an hungred, and ye gave me meat: I was thirsty, and ye gave me drink: I was a stranger, and ye took me in:

2. Psalm 39:12 Hear my prayer, O LORD, and give ear unto my cry; hold not thy peace at my tears: for I am a stranger with thee, and a sojourner, as all my fathers were.

3. John 8:23 And he said unto them, Ye are from beneath; I am from above: ye are of this world; I am not of this world.

4. Luke 4:4, 8, 12 (4) And Jesus answered him, saying, It is written, That man shall not live by bread alone, but by every word of God. (8) And Jesus answered and said unto him, Get thee behind me, Satan: for it is written, Thou shalt worship the Lord thy God, and him only shalt thou serve. (12) And Jesus answering said unto him, It is said, Thou shalt not tempt the Lord thy God.

Battlefield Tactics

1. John 8:44 Ye are of your father the devil, and the lusts of your father ye will do. He was a murderer from the beginning, and abode not in the truth, because there is no truth in him. When he speaketh a lie, he speaketh of his own: for he is a liar, and the father of it.

2. Revelation 12:10 And I heard a loud voice saying in heaven, Now is come salvation, and strength, and the kingdom of our God, and the power of his Christ: for the accuser of our brethren is cast down, which accused them before our God day and night.

3. Matthew 12:24 But when the Pharisees heard it, they said, This fellow doth not cast out devils, but by Beelzebub the prince of the devils.

4. Ephesians 2:2 Wherein in time past ye walked according to the course of this world, according to the prince of the power of the air, the spirit that now worketh in the children of disobedience:

5.	Ephesians 6:12 For we wrestle not against flesh and blood, but against principalities, against powers, against the rulers of the darkness of this world, against spiritual wickedness in high places.

6.	Matthew 12:43 When the unclean spirit is gone out of a man, he walketh through dry places, seeking rest, and findeth none.

7.	Matthew 13:19 When any one heareth the word of the kingdom, and understandeth it not, then cometh the wicked one, and catcheth away that which was sown in his heart. This is he which received seed by the way side.

8.	Matthew 13:39 The enemy that sowed them is the devil; the harvest is the end of the world; and the reapers are the angels.

9.	John 12:31 Now is the judgment of this world: now shall the prince of this world be cast out.

10.	John 14:30 Hereafter I will not talk much with you: for the prince of this world cometh, and hath nothing in me.

11.	Ephesians 2:2 Wherein in time past ye walked according to the course of this world, according to the prince of the power of the air, the spirit that now worketh in the children of disobedience.

Coming Home/War's End

1.	2 Corinthians 11:22-33 22 Are they Hebrews? so am I. Are they Israelites? so am I. Are they the seed of Abraham? so am I. Are they ministers of Christ? (I speak as a fool) I am more; in labours more abundant, in stripes above measure, in prisons more frequent, in deaths oft. Of the Jews five times received I forty stripes save one. Thrice was I beaten with rods, once was I stoned, thrice I suffered shipwreck, a night and a day I have been in the deep; In journeyings often, in perils of waters, in perils of robbers, in perils by mine own countrymen, in perils by the heathen, in perils in the city, in perils in the wilderness, in perils in the sea, in perils among false brethren; In weariness and painfulness, in watchings often, in hunger and thirst, in fastings often, in cold and nakedness. Beside those things that are without, that which cometh upon me daily, the care of all the churches. Who is weak, and I am not weak? who is offended, and I burn not? If I must needs glory, I will glory of the things which concern mine infirmities. The God and Father of our Lord Jesus Christ, which is blessed for evermore, knoweth that I lie not. In Damascus the governor under Aretas the king kept the city of the Damascenes with a garrison, desirous to apprehend me: And through a window in a basket was I let down by the wall, and escaped his hands.

2. Revelation 19:11-16 And I saw heaven opened, and behold a white horse; and he that sat upon him was called Faithful and True, and in righteousness he doth judge and make war. His eyes were as a flame of fire, and on his head were many crowns; and he had a name written, that no man knew, but he himself. And he was clothed with a vesture dipped in blood: and his name is called The Word of God. And the armies which were in heaven followed him upon white horses, clothed in fine linen, white and clean. And out of his mouth goeth a sharp sword, that with it he should smite the nations: and he shall rule them with a rod of iron: and he treadeth the winepress of the fierceness and wrath of Almighty God. And he hath on his vesture and on his thigh a name written, KING OF KINGS, AND LORD OF LORDS.

3. Revelation 20:1-3 And I saw an angel come down from heaven, having the key of the bottomless pit and a great chain in his hand. And he laid hold on the dragon, that old serpent, which is the Devil, and Satan, and bound him a thousand years, And cast him into the bottomless pit, and shut him up, and set a seal upon him,

that he should deceive the nations no more, till the thousand years should be fulfilled: and after that he must be loosed a little season

4. Isaiah 2:4 And he shall judge among the nations, and shall rebuke many people: and they shall beat their swords into plowshares, and their spears into pruninghooks: nation shall not lift up sword against nation, neither shall they learn war any more.

5. Isaiah 9:7 Of the increase of his government and peace there shall be no end, upon the throne of David, and upon his kingdom, to order it, and to establish it with judgment and with justice from henceforth even for ever. The zeal of the LORD of hosts will perform this.

6. Isaiah 29:17-19 Is it not yet a very little while, and Lebanon shall be turned into a fruitful field, and the fruitful field shall be esteemed as a forest? And in that day shall the deaf hear the words of the book, and the eyes of the blind shall see out of obscurity, and out of darkness. The meek also shall increase their joy in the LORD, and the poor among men shall rejoice in the Holy One of Israel.

7. Isaiah 33:24 And the inhabitant shall not say, I am sick: the people that dwell therein shall be forgiven their iniquity.

8. Isaiah 30:23 Then shall he give the rain of thy seed, that thou shalt sow the ground withal; and bread of the increase of the earth, and it shall be fat and plenteous: in that day shall thy cattle feed in large pastures.

9. Joel 2:21-27 Fear not, O land; be glad and rejoice: for the LORD will do great things. Be not afraid, ye beasts of the field: for the pastures of the wilderness do spring, for the tree beareth her fruit, the fig tree and the vine do yield their strength. Be glad then, ye children of Zion, and rejoice in the LORD your God: for he hath given you the former rain moderately, and he will cause to come

down for you the rain, the former rain, and the latter rain in the first month. And the floors shall be full of wheat, and the vats shall overflow with wine and oil. And I will restore to you the years that the locust hath eaten, the cankerworm, and the caterpillar, and the palmerworm, my great army which I sent among you. And ye shall eat in plenty, and be satisfied, and praise the name of the LORD your God, that hath dealt wondrously with you: and my people shall never be ashamed. And ye shall know that I am in the midst of Israel, and that I am the LORD your God, and none else: and my people shall never be ashamed.

10. Isaiah 45:23 I have sworn by myself, the word is gone out of my mouth in righteousness, and shall not return, That unto me every knee shall bow, every tongue shall swear.

11. Zephaniah 3:9 For then will I turn to the people a pure language, that they may all call upon the name of the LORD, to serve him with one consent.

12. Revelation 20:10-15 10 And the devil that deceived them was cast into the lake of fire and brimstone, where the beast and the false prophet are, and shall be tormented day and night for ever and ever. And I saw a great white throne, and him that sat on it, from whose face the earth and the heaven fled away; and there was found no place for them. And I saw the dead, small and great, stand before God; and the books were opened: and another book was opened, which is the book of life: and the dead were judged out of those things which were written in the books, according to their works. And the sea gave up the dead which were in it; and death and hell delivered up the dead which were in them: and they were judged every man according to their works. And death and hell were cast into the lake of fire. This is the second death. And whosoever was not found written in the book of life was cast into the lake of fire.

Enclosures

Enclosure 1

Example – Rules of Engagement

Rules of Engagement
Joint Task Force for Somalia Relief Operations
Ground Forces

Nothing in these rules of engagement limits your right to take appropriate action to defend yourself and your unit.

1. You have the right to use force to defend yourself against attacks or threats of attack.

2. Hostile fire may be returned effectively and promptly to stop a hostile act.

3. When US forces are attacked by *unarmed* hostile elements, mobs, and/or rioters, U.S. forces should use the minimum force necessary under the circumstances and proportional to the threat.

4. You may not seize the property of others to accomplish your mission.

5. Detention of civilians is authorized for security reasons or in self-defense.

Remember

- The United States is **not** at war.

- Treat all persons with dignity and respect.

- Use minimum force to carry out the mission.

- Always be prepared to act in self-defense.

Enclosure 2

Example - Discipleship training subjects:

- **Bibliology:** The organization, canonization, and preservation of the Bible.

- **Salvation:** A study of the process by which man is delivered from condemnation to eternal life with Jesus Christ.

- **Assurance of Salvation**: How to know for sure that you're "saved" and going to heaven.

- **The Trinity**: A study of the Godhead. God is one Being but exists in three separate persons, God the Father, Jesus Christ, and the Holy Spirit.

- **The Church**: A study of the New Testament church, its importance, purpose, organization, and leadership.

- **Prayer**: A study of why we pray, how to pray, when to pray, and the hindrances to prayer.

- **Growing in Christ**: A study on how to have a more personal relationship with God.

- **Witnessing**: How to lead others to the saving grace of Jesus Christ.

- **Bible Doctrines:** To introduce the student to the field of systematic theology and to give him a general understanding of the cardinal doctrines of the Word of God.

Enclosure 3

The Soldiers Creed:

I am an American Soldier.
I am a Warrior and a member of a team.
I serve the people of the United States, and live the Army Values.
I will always place the mission first.
I will never accept defeat.
I will never quit.
I will never leave a fallen comrade.
I am disciplined, physically and mentally tough, trained and proficient in my warrior tasks and drills.
I always maintain my arms, my equipment and myself.
I am an expert and I am a professional.
I stand ready to deploy, engage, and destroy, the enemies of the United States of America in close combat.
I am a guardian of freedom and the American way of life.
I am an American Soldier.

Enclosure 4

The 91ˢᵗ Psalm

He that dwelleth in the secret place of the most High shall abide under the shadow of the Almighty. I will say of the LORD, He is my refuge and my fortress: my God; in him will I trust. Surely he shall deliver thee from the snare of the fowler, and from the noisome pestilence. He shall cover thee with his feathers, and under his wings shalt thou trust: his truth shall be thy shield and buckler. Thou shalt not be afraid for the terror by night; nor for the arrow that flieth by day; Nor for the pestilence that walketh in darkness; nor for the destruction that wasteth at noonday. A thousand shall fall at thy side, and ten thousand at thy right hand; but it shall not come nigh thee. Only with thine eyes shalt thou behold and see the reward of the wicked. Because thou hast made the LORD, which is my refuge, even the most High, thy habitation; There shall no evil befall thee, neither shall any plague come nigh thy dwelling. For he shall give his angels charge over thee, to keep thee in all thy ways. They shall bear thee up in their hands, lest thou dash thy foot against a stone. Thou shalt tread upon the lion and adder: the young lion and the dragon shalt thou trample under feet. Because he hath set his love upon me, therefore will I deliver him: I will set him on high, because he hath known my name. He shall call upon me, and I will answer him: I will be with him in trouble; I will deliver him, and honour him. With long life will I satisfy him, and shew him my salvation.

CPSIA information can be obtained
at www.ICGtesting.com
Printed in the USA
FSHW010149121021
85358FS

9 781478 724674